The Footwear Industry

The
Footwear
Industry:
Profiles in
Leadership

Edited by Richard L. Cohen

FAIRCHILD PUBLICATIONS, INC.

NEW YORK

Dedicated to

Charles Silversmith.

1938–1966

Contents

Introduction

THE interviews in this book are really stop-action word-and-picture photographs of varying candidness, depending on the executive's willingness to hold still and face the camera. These articles were all written during the second half of the 1960's, years of unprecedented affluence for the American economy and the footwear industry. The period represented something more for an historic industry whose responsibility it is to shod the American nation.

The sixties, from the foreshortened prospective of proximity, seem linch pin years during which an industry, steeped in tradition, pivoted slowly into a new era, a new way of looking at itself and its society.

The changes that occurred were compounded of many conditions. Each had some impact—cosmic in some cases, modest in others—on both the companies of this industry and the men who ran those companies.

From the standpoint of production, a major impact resulted from the antitrust judgment of 1955 which required United Shoe Machinery Corp. to sell, as well as lease, its machines to shoe producers. The decision paved the way for the introduction of new manufacturing technologies, and offered the hope that one of the last mass-production industries heavily dependent on hand work might, in the not-too-distant future, use machines instead of men to do its routine, repetitive work.

Without going into the exceedingly complex economic considerations on which the 1955 United Shoe decree was based, it is enough to recall the oft-mentioned view of footwear manufacturers: that the ruling opened the shoe machinery market to innovation—and innovate it did, with unprecedented vigor and variety.

But the footwear industry, in its essence, is not a production-oriented industry; it is a consumer-oriented industry, highly sensitive (when its antennae are functioning properly) to shifts in the public's tastes and appetites. It is to satisfy these appetites that footwear production is primarily directed.

During this period of change, two aspects of American life were revolutionized: affluence of the nation, and mobility of its citizenry.

The nation had achieved a degree of affluence that had been unforeseen by most. And the population was literally upended and on the move—a mobility that shook, and eventually shattered, the foundations on which the business of distributing footwear to the public had been confidently built.

Like American industry in general, the footwear industry had historically been oriented to an economy of scarcity. It saw itself providing one of life's basics—like potatoes or electric power.

Competition in the marketplace meant, in the final analysis, price competition. The consumer, for the most part, was seen as motivated by price considerations almost exclusively.

The central consideration was: how much does it cost? Not, what other satisfactions might it afford? (A retired head of Thom McAn, the nation's largest retail chain, used to say that if his company raised or lowered prices by a penny, the reaction would be felt immediately in increased or decreased sales: they don't say that at Thom McAn anymore.)

The change was glacier-like in importance. It affected the entire footwear production industry. No longer was price king—it was still very important, but not the all-powerful consideration. New qualities hard to grapple with, hard to fathom—like personal taste and emotional satisfaction—became matters of great significance to an awakened industry.

Then, the impact of mobility. Main Street, along with center-city shopping habits, moved to the suburbs. A subject of conversation since the end of World War II, it now became a marketing and merchandising reality to footwear executives. Out of the old decayed "main street" shopping districts arose cries for urban renewal and a scramble to lease space in shopping centers.

The shift in population and business left wreckage in its wake. Not only the small, independent retailer, but large, presumably sophisticated multi-unit corporations, struggled to stay alive. Companies, large and small, that spotted the marketing changes, prospered. Those that didn't have their stories recorded in Chapter XI archives, or survived by the skin of their lightest shoes.

Other changes left their marks in the mid-sixties:

● The Brown Shoe antitrust decision of 1962 put a limit, however indefinable, on the acquisition of smaller companies by giants.

● The enormous growth in popularity of the sneaker in all its variations, proving that the American footwear market was not the exclusive preserve of leather footwear.

● The great flood of imported footwear of all types, demonstrating that non-American footwear manufacturers were fully capable of exploiting the rich, American market.

The executives whose stories appear in this book dealt successfully and often shaped these changes. These men, it can be fairly stated, represent the cream of a major American industry—with all the brilliance, imperiousness, eccentricity, leadership, shrewdness and dynamism that might reasonably be expected from such a diverse group of individuals.

Their one real bond is that they are all prominent members of a community, in this case the footwear community. As such, they can be offered with pride, as the best of their community.

Millions of printed words to the contrary notwithstanding, prominent and successful businessmen are not particularly easy to interview. Their prominence tends to make them guarded; they are inclined by the traditions of business strategy to mask their moves, hold their cards close to their chests.

It is to their credit—and to the credit of the reporters on *Footwear News,* a Fairchild Publications weekly newspaper, which printed the interviews initially—that so much of their beliefs, experiences and personalities were revealed.

They cover the spectrum of business executives of the 1960's. There are the elder statesmen, men like Joseph Stern, Sr., of United States Shoe Corp., who, with fierce and uncompromising will, built the giant United States Shoe Corp. out of a moribund manufacturing plant. In contrast is Francis Rooney, the young president of Melville Shoe Corp., the largest retail footwear company, who sees himself as a professional manager, bringing to his company not the gifts of the footwear expert, but the rationally developed skills of the management executive.

There is David Evins, who has combined the flamboyant talents of the shoe designer with the quiet acumen of the businessman, and who has made the often chancey business of high fashion a profitable career. At another point on the circle of footwear executives is the imperturbable E. Morton Jennings, Jr., who is, strictly speaking, not a shoeman, but a banker. But he has spent a lifetime lending money (sometimes refusing to lend money) to the footwear industry and has viewed its changes from a unique vantage point. John Reinhart, who has brought to the business of making infants' footwear all the weapons of marketing strategy that are usually associated with high velocity products as toothpaste and detergents. Clifford O. Anderson, who started his career as an engineer, and who, through the happenstance of corporate reorganizations in the depression years of the 1930's, found himself put to work building the bankrupt G. R. Kinney Co. into a powerful company that reflected his own towering and strong-willed personality.

A note on method. Future historians of the Age of the Press Agent and Image-Builder should record that none of the interviews was originally suggested by the executive or his company, and only two asked to have public relations advisors present. No interview was ever submitted before publication. The executives saw the finished product in *Footwear News*.

The object of the interviews was not to publish full-length personal and business biographies of these 23 executives, or to describe how their friends and enemies in the footwear industry regarded them, but rather to present them, and their essential juices, at a given moment in time. The interviewers tried to avoid spreading a great deal of material thinly; they concentrated on exploring in depth some facet of the man's career, or company, or his role in the economic structure of the industry. At times, the executive talked of matters that were uppermost in his mind; in other situations, interviewers carefully guided the discussion to throw illumination on what they considered to be the salient aspects of the executive's career.

The executives, with a few obvious exceptions, are outstanding examples of that breed of man whose extinction is chronically forecast, the entrepreneur. The term cuts across ages, positions and the ownership stake in the business. These executives are characteristically inventive, quick to decide and act, pragmatic, flexible and are possessed of a sure instinct for cutting through to the bone of a situation. They are talented money-makers. They are vigorous and vastly self-assured. They work hard and discuss their work with evident relish. They are builders.

The interviews appear here as originally published, with the exception that errors have been corrected, and operating figures have been updated to the latest available at the time of publication, unless otherwise stated in the text.

Richard L. Cohen

New York, N.Y.
November, 1966

Part One

The Charismatic Executive

CHAPTER 1
Big Man at Kinney

Clifford O.
Anderson

A SLIDE RULE is a third arm to Clifford O. Anderson, president of Kinney Shoe Corp. . . . he always has one around. "I couldn't operate without this tool. It helps me to analyze, check figures, relate sales to inventory and gives a quick guide to percentages."

He is a man driven to know what's going on and he wants quick answers. Speed is important to a man who operates a business that had sales of $120 million by the end of 1965, has over 700 stores and 6 factories. A big jump from the $53 million volume of 10 years ago.

His 17th floor office is liberally sprinkled with memorabilia of Abraham Lincoln. A framed photo and handwritten letter hang on one wall, a large bronze replica of the Lincoln penny is on a shelf, and etchings of the 16th President are on the other walls.

He admires Lincoln and would most certainly blush if one tried to compare him with the log splitter from Illinois, even though he too comes from a poor family, stands 6 feet, 4 inches, achieved fame and fortune, has a deep sense of social responsibility and, most important of all, possesses the inquisitiveness of mind that so often leads to success.

In soft tones he reveals his deep feelings for people when he tells how "last year we opened a plant in Beaver Springs, Pa., a depressed area and we gave steady 52 weeks-a-year employment to people in need of help." (Only then does he add details on how the factory has the latest and most efficient equipment available.)

"People are important, they're not just pieces of machinery that keep a firm functioning. My parents were immigrants from Sweden, and they were poor. My father was a tailor and was out of work as much as 5 months a year during the slack summer periods. I know what hard times can mean.

"That's why I have worked so hard to make this company a success. I feel a personal responsibility to develop Kinney, not just because of the company, but because it is an important part of industry and the total American economy. I'm grateful that we can open 60 stores a year, because they mean jobs and nothing makes a guy like me happier."

Swiveling his chair to face the conference table that fronts his desk, Mr. Anderson then proceeds to expound his views on what makes a company (not just a shoe company) successful.

"It's people, executives, company personnel who are properly trained and yet who can think for themselves. No one man is indispensible. For long term success a company must have depth of management in all age brackets.

"Industry has a multitude of men who are good administrators. What we lack are men who are dynamic . . . who see growth as a way of life and are not just concerned with plain day-to-day living. There aren't too many people like this. When you see a business that is leveling off it means that there is an absence of qualified men in the company. That's why management is our keystone to success."

There is no doubt that Kinney has been successful. For many years it has been the wonder child of the shoe industry, wooed and pursued by any number of companies.

Just how active the pursuit has been can best be described by Mr. Anderson.

"When George Smith was president (Mr. Smith died in 1959) and I was executive vice-president, no less than half-a-dozen companies wanted to merge with us.

"Any number of companies were interested, but their only concern seemed to be in our balance sheets. George and I had some long talks with Clark Gamble (chairman of Brown Shoe Co.) to discuss a possible merger. We were delighted because Clark had a different attitude from the other people we talked to. Of course he was interested in our profit picture, but his chief concern was in our executive structure and the people we had. (Brown merged with Kinney in 1956.)

"We pointed out to Clark that we were a successful company because we were individualistic, and that if we were to be dominated by Brown then no merger was possible. Clark's answer was, 'We're interested in Kinney because of its management team and policies and there won't be any interference from us in its operations.'

"George and I then talked with the heads of other companies that had merged with Brown and they said the same thing. Well, during all our years with Brown we operated exactly as when we were alone. But Brown was extremely helpful in our factory division where we were weak compared with Brown's factory strength."

Patting back his steel gray hair, Mr. Anderson continued . . . "Six years later when Woolworth's bought us the same topic came up. (In June 1962, the U. S. Supreme Court ordered Brown to divest itself of Kinney, and Woolworth purchased the chain in 1963.) During our first meeting with the top people of Woolworth the discussion was devoted to our management and its depth and strength of character.

"I told Bob Kirkwood (chairman of Woolworth) that we would have to operate as an independent subsidiary. His answer was that Woolworth wanted Kinney for its management and individualism, because they realized that the shoe business was very complicated and they knew little about it.

"During the last 3 years there has never been any interference in the management of Kinney's affairs, just cooperative translation of ideas. Woolworth's is a wonderful source of capital, but so far there has been no need to call on them because we are generating it in our own operations. We now open 60–65 stores yearly and a factory every year and a half."

Asked what he looks for when hiring men, Cliff leaned back in his chair and thought for a moment. "We look for a lot of things. When we hire a man for our New York office he must be a college graduate, have thinking ability, absorptive qualities, a desire to listen and learn, a base from which he can project himself and imaginative creative energies. He must make us feel he can grow. He can't be the caboose on our train but rather the sparkplug."

To develop this creative feeling in all levels of management he holds monthly meetings of the 18 top executives of the chain. Each man exposes his operation completely, so everyone knows what's going on. "We also have about 20 other men sitting in, often young men who have just joined Kinney. A question and answer period follows and everybody, especially the young men, are exposed to the intimate details of the business and this creates immediate growth in their minds.

"We try to keep our executives from falling into a pattern of sameness. We want young men because youth is revolutionary. It comes up with new ideas. No matter how crazy these ideas may seem they often hold a germ that we can latch on to. We don't want a man to do a job, but one who thinks beyond it. We require it, encourage it and get it."

Reflecting on what depth of management has meant to Kinney over the years since he joined it in 1931 as purchasing agent, Anderson points out that, "I came in during the depression. I know what can happen to a badly managed company that relies on old time sameness. We had to change that. We had more liabilities than assets. The thinking and tempo of operation of its people had to change. Young men were brought in, trained, given an opportunity to develop themselves and offer new ideas.

"When I first came to Kinney the retail stores had to take everything the factories turned out regardless of price, style or whether the merchandise was in demand. There was no competitive feeling. Now our factories must compete with outside manufacturers for our retail business. We don't give our factories business for sentimental reasons. When the factory men come in to see our buyers, they may be the greatest of friends, but their prices, styles and quality must be competitive, or we don't buy from them."

A City College graduate (A.B. 1922), he now stands as one of the shining lights of the school. President of the Alumni Association, toastmaster at the 90th birthday dinner of the late Bernard Baruch, he holds many awards for his contributions to the school. His proudest award may be a paperweight on his desk which reads, "To Cliff Anderson with deep affection from his CCNY Class of 1922, presented April 18, 1958."

A frequent speaker at industry affairs, he was also president of the Volume Footwear Retailers' Association; a director of Woolworth's and the Glen Ridge N. J. Trust Co., just to keep him busy in his spare time.

Looking at the state of shoe chain business in general, he says, "Chain stores are entering an era of profitable expansion. Now chains are pricing merchandise to the market, which is not down but up. Chains reached their low point several years ago when many leading chains dropped their prices hoping for more business. Now they recognize the consumer market and are pricing their goods to it, and now chain stores are a profitable business."

Returning to Kinney, he admitted that boutique operations don't appeal to management at this moment. Most stores are just large enough for the wide selection of family shoes they offer. "But this doesn't mean that if the shoe business begins to sag that we wouldn't think in terms of other merchandise."

Right now Kinney concentrates its operations in four directions, downtown, shopping centers, free standing stores and leased departments. But Mr. Anderson sees a particular future in leased departments in good promotional department stores (he stresses the word good). "We are not committed to shoe stores as the only area in which to sell shoes; we will sell shoes wherever customers want to go."

He doesn't think that good promotional stores will take over their leased shoe departments because such operations require special professional shoe experience. "Look at Macy's and Burdine's."

Why must Kinney compete for the leased shoe sections in Woolco stores owned by Woolworth and is possible antitrust action the reason? "No, antitrust doesn't enter the picture, but there is a good business reason. This is a highly competitive market and competition keeps everyone on his toes. If our factories compete for our business, why shouldn't we compete for Woolco leases."

Next question: Does Kinney plan any outside acquisitions? "No, we plan to expand from within and have been pretty successful so far."

Why did you try to acquire Weyenberg Shoe Manufacturing Co. "We were interested in its growth potential and because it operated in a high price area that we weren't active in." (The Justice Department wouldn't give its approval to the deal and it fell through.)

Mr. Anderson has a second thought. "There is another area where we are expanding. Canada has a lot of potential. We plan to grow throughout Canada and will have a 100 per cent Canadian operation, with Canadian personnel, as soon as the people are trained. His son Richard is president of the new operation. "I didn't pick Richard, Dick Stewart, vice-president, did. I don't believe in nepotism. I don't recommend that a son get into the same business as his father's because the son then has a very rough road to hack. Harder than if he weren't related." Another son, Clifford, is in the public and community relations department of J. C. Penney, Inc.

In 1968 he is scheduled to step down from the helm and he honestly hopes he won't be missed.

"I'm opposed to one man rule. I've been one of the most active supporters of compulsory retirement at 65. There is nothing finer for your management team than for your executives to know that the firm's top posts will be vacated when their holders reach 65. It gives capable, aggressive men something to shoot for."

No one is being groomed for his job. All his top men know the ins and outs of all aspects of the business. "As a man grows older his efforts tend to level off. If you groom a man for a certain job and he starts to level off, then you have problems and bitterness, if he has to be replaced."

From 1922 to 1928, he was a professional basketball player (he has the height for it). Does he still play basketball? "No, I was born in 1903, I couldn't play the game at my age." What does he plan to do when he retires? Golf several times a week, swim, read the books he had no time for before, travel slowly around the world studying his favorite subjects . . . people.

He will continue to collect hand carved figures, a collection of which holds prominent space in his office. "My wife and I also collect Royal Doulton pieces. Once in London we stopped at the firm's office and found we had a larger variety of items than they had on display."

"I plan a complete retirement from business." (Certain friends claim he won't be able to.)

In the back of his mind is the hope that he can lecture

at some leading college "because the experience I've accu-
mulated over the years could be helpful to students. After
all, I originally planned to be a teacher."

CHAPTER 2

The Fine Art of Building
a Modest Empire

Harold O.
Toor

"I'M A MAN with a mission in a hurry. I'm a dreamer: I think when I lie in bed before falling asleep—'Imagine the effect of opening high-grade men's shoe stores in large cities all over the country.' "

Harold Oliver Toor recently allowed a visitor a peek at one of his fantasies, a rare glimpse of that part of him that is the dreamer. But the sixtyish president of Freeman-Toor Corp., merged in 1966 with U. S. Shoe Corp., displays many other parts too, and their sum is a highly skilled financial engineer who has used his specialized understanding of footwear industry subtleties to advance to the front rank in the industry.

Hal Toor, chairman of U. S. Shoe, also heads the $35 plus million (sales) parent of Freeman Shoe Co. (manufacturer and retailer of men's footwear with over 300 leased departments in high-grade men's apparel stores and four of its own stores); H. O. Toor Shoe Corp. (manufacturer of infants' and children's cements, boys' welts and men's welts and casuals) and Chesapeake Shoe Manufacturing Corp. (children's and boys' welts and cements). It makes private label children's footwear and owns the names of James A. Banister Co., high-grade men's maker.

Toor at leisure labors as intensely as Toor at work. His pleasures include opera and collecting contemporary art. He and his wife are patrons of the Metropolitan Opera and part of the Toor art collection hangs about him in his office; some occasionally dress up new Freeman departments for a time.

On his business-side Toor has almost single-handedly built a multimillion-dollar corporation, and is presently making final additions to its relatively new staff of professional managers prior to becoming a publicly-owned company next year.

To get where he has is an achievement that would have satisfied other men his age sufficiently to slow their pace. A recent mild heart attack has both his wife and his doctor telephoning him these days to remind him to take things easy. He sits like a lion leashed, but keeps wheeling. As he says, he's a dreamer who has a mission.

Toor wonders whether he's taking the role of an industry elder statesman—he isn't sure. But he sat back and reflected like one, his mind quick and sharp.

You've been accused of not being able to delegate authority and responsibility, of holding on, of being a one-man company.

"The accusation was true, originally. By the time I acquired H. Jacob & Sons," (the forerunner of H. O. Toor Shoe Corp. bought during the 1930's) I did everything myself. Why not? I had time enough and more. But when I expanded more I saw the value of developing talent in men."

"We need men's factories mostly but we want other companies, if they fit in. We expect to enlarge and we're not prevented from considering firms other than men's shoe companies or shoe firms themselves."

How do you size-up a company for merger?

"You've got to know arithmetic, for one thing. But you need to know people too. You ask yourself if it fits in. Do we have the management to run it, or do they? No one turns down good management. Manpower is the important thing today. Management comes first and finances come second, because any successful company can get all the financial assistance it needs."

What are your management problems?

"Most of our people have been trained from within. But our growth has been so rapid we haven't been able to supply all our needs. So we had to go outside for both our financial

and marketing vice-presidents, and in the near future we
expect to name a vice-president from the outside who will
be responsible for purchasing. Our two biggest problems are
getting enough good managers and enough production."

*Which are the meaningful financial indicators in the shoe
business?*

"The percentage of profit on sales is the barometer on the
industry today. You don't disregard return on invested capital but in the shoe business I think return on dollar-sale is
more important for this reason: The shoe industry is more
reliant on labor than it is on plant investment."

What is the trick to marketing men's fashion?

"There's been a big swing toward apparel store distribution and there's nothing to stop it from going further. New
stores will open with shoe departments and others are being
added now. The new stores now provide the space in advance. Before that the business was in men's shoe stores,
which superseded family stores in the larger cities. But the
greatest growth area is in the apparel stores.

"We find that unlike the popular-price sections which may
attract a man off the street, in the high-grade business we get
his purchase when he buys a suit. Therefore, our shoe departments are near the suit sections.

"The men's clothing industry has made men more fashion
conscious—the shoe industry alone hasn't and couldn't have.
I think fashion became more important as the standard of
living changed and people got tired of the sloppy look. The
casual look is much neater now and men have begun to look
at shoes along with clothes. They've been awakened to style.
Dressing well today is a status symbol.

"This growth in apparel stores has made everyone more

shoe conscious. The brand lines have improved and increased their advertising and I think this also has done quite a bit to awaken the American male."

Where is men's footwear fashion headed?

"Lightweight, flexible shoes are here to stay for a long time because men have found them to be comfortable. And I can understand why, because we control our environment more and more. We're warm in the winter and cool in the summer.

"And more casual footwear has been developing. Not cheap casuals to compete with sneakers. I mean good casuals —$15 and up. Twenty dollars is a good price for the $30 dress shoe buyer—he's in that category, but I see no reason why he won't pay $25.

"Color is important in this respect: Even if you don't sell it, you attract with it and arouse interest, get exposure."

How does one lease a men's shoe department in a clothing store?

"Today most operators of men's apparel stores are trying to offer complete wardrobes, meaning footwear too. So the stores without shoes are looking for them.

"We analyze the store—appraise the volume and see whether it's profitable for us to go in. We tailor the sales approach to the individual store. The percentage we pay has to remain confidential, but there's no rule of thumb. You must take into consideration the kind of store and the nature of the city.

"We're trying a new approach in some Freeman departments—a salon type, with no exposed boxes. It's sort of a club-room atmosphere similar to what's been done in women's. This is a high-grade, high-class approach."

How important is fitting in the children's high-volume, low-price field?

"Fitting is important, but retailers in both the high-end and popular-price fields pay too much attention to fit. People who go in and try on shoes themselves are fitted just as well.

"Fit should be important. This applies to women and children—men are more meticulous about fit and are fitted better. Children's shoes are made to fit and then it depends on the clerk. I think less attention is paid to fit in the volume category but they don't pay too much attention in the higher grade sometimes.

"To say that style ruins children's feet is a gross exaggeration. More attention is paid to fit where the mother controls the purchase, but the necessity for fit was much greater when people walked more, and even kids don't walk as much. I think children should be properly fitted but no one can prove to me that children are being fitted any worse than they've been in the past.

"Men are more interested in fit—they find a last they like and they stay with it. Men will sacrifice style for fit, something few women will do. That's why men will buy the higher grades, because they can get both."

What is the future of controlled distribution?

"Controlled distribution is very important. It doesn't mean the disappearance of individual manufacturers who make shoes only for the trade. But the big push, as at Brown and International, indicates that controlled distribution is essential. For Florsheim it's in their stores. In our case it's in leased departments."

Toor made a quick hand gesture to check his watch and rose abruptly. "Let's have lunch," he said, already headed for the door. Soon the 37th floor of the Empire State Building was behind and Hal Toor hosted lunch at the building's Empire State Club, of which he is a director.

Forceful, serious, outgoing, Toor has an activist attitude toward shoe industry affairs. He has always picked a spot close to the action. His public work for the shoe industry goes back to 1933, when he was a member of the shoe code authority under NRA. He has relinquished several committee posts, he says, because of his company's growth, but until this year he flew often between his New York headquarters and Washington on industry business. More recently he was president of the National Footwear Manufacturers' Association.

Back on the 37th floor after lunch, Toor led the way back through the carpeted executive suite. The pastel corridors serve as a backdrop for more of the Toor art collection, spotted around the office.

So on past his private secretary's office into his own—a luxurious room with a comfortable couch and chairs, deep-cushioned carpeting and a sweeping view of New York looking south from 34th Street and Fifth Avenue, 37 stories high. Brooklyn and Queens loom to the left and Wall Street is dead ahead. New Jersey is foggy to the right but all of lower Fifth Avenue is clear.

A bronze plaque near his desk reads, "Nothing will ever be attempted if all possible objections must first be overcome." The words fit Toor's actions, yet the statement comes not from him but from someone very like him. The signature is that of Nathan Cummings, chairman, Consolidated Foods Corp., Toor's son-in-law.

Toor settled back and, appearing slightly tired, prepared for more questions.

How has technology affected the industry?

"In a very important way. In the old days the executives knew technology—they came up through the ranks: Worker to foreman to executive. Today you need engineers: Plant engineers for plant layout and others for other technological improvements which must be investigated, must be tried out.

"But we don't want group manufacturing—we want quality. Our conveyors only transport racks. In some automated operations the whole thing is dependent on the slowest man. Ours don't require this kind of teamwork.

"Heat-sealing may have a place, but it eliminates some fancy stitching that's very stylish. It turns out very plain shoes.

"Automation will separate further the high grade and low. In quality footwear you'll always need to pay more attention."

Trade associations seem to be playing a different role these days. They used to be defensive in their actions but are now consciously seeking change. Why has the focus of interest shifted?

"There must be a justification for the existence of a trade association because they require time and money from their members. In order to justify that existence they have to offer something other than just a shoe show.

"So the seminars, for example, were started and proved to be quite effective. The man we sent from Freeman said he got a lot out of it.

"Our associations have to play a more important part in Washington because people in business need information about things that go on there that affect their businesses. And the best way to get it is through their associations.

"The role of a trade group is to keep alert and to know everything that's going on and to protect the interest of the people they represent. I think ours have done a pretty good job in this respect.

"Activity in itself is not new but the National Footwear Manufacturers' Association became more active because it thought such activity was more important. This started about 10 years ago when the role of technology changed. The NFMA needed and got a technical man and had a technical viewpoint."

Has the industry still an import problem?

"Yes, to some degree it still does. When I went to Italy and to Washington to fight against imports it wasn't a personal thing. After all, Freeman buys imports for its departments. Even so, with the tight labor situation in America I don't know if we could make all the shoes we sell."

CHAPTER 3

12.6 Per Cent on Sales; 21.4 Per Cent on Capital: He Must Be Doing Something Right

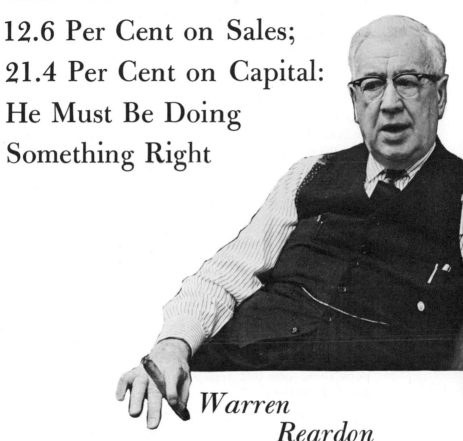

Warren Reardon

WARREN REARDON, 74-year-old president of Daniel Green Co.—at Dolgeville in sleepy upstate New York—says most of the time at home he goes barefoot, except for a ragged pair of slippers he wears to keep his feet warm on the cold bathroom tile while he's shaving.

Not so barefoot is the $1 million-plus net earnings after taxes in 1966, on the $8,673,893 volume the men's and women's slipper company did. Or the fact that 28 of its 36 styles accounted for 97 per cent of sales.

For it is Warren Reardon who sets the pace for the footwear industry in profit as a per cent of sales—12.6 per cent in 1966—and his company is among the leaders in profit as a per cent of invested capital, 21.4 per cent in 1966. (He is also reported to be the grey eminence as a director of Endicott Johnson Corp., shaping that company's path behind the scenes.)

Dolgeville is some 200 miles northwest of Manhattan. Its air is clean. Its streets are clean. The houses look freshly scraped and painted. Main Street is dominated by a big grey stone, somewhat forbidding, building that used to be Alfred Dolge's piano felt factory, but is now Green's main office building and warehousing facility.

Nearby is an old opera house. It is Green's "Factory No. 2." Remnants of a once-luxurious parquet floor can be seen in portions of the production area. Adjacent in a wood-frame building—once Dolge's stables—is "Factory No. 1."

It is safe to say Dolgeville's economy is dominated by the company in the grey stone building. About one fifth of its population, some 602 persons, work for Daniel Green Co. A King's Row town.

True to fiction expectations, Reardon and his wife "ramble around" in a 33-room Victorian mansion built by the long-late Dolge—who is sort of a folk hero in these parts because he brought electricity here before Albany got it, built an opera house and instituted the first industrial noncontributory pension plan, before he blew his wad on a hairbrain scheme to build a short-run railroad to nearby Little Falls.

658.98 C66
c.1

But what's this? What's Reardon saying?

"In this business you've got to stay beyond the designers. We used to hire the best European designers on a retainer basis. I hired (Elsa) Schiaparelli before anyone had ever heard of her . . . Her stuff was too wild for us . . . Now we pay on royalty . . . Just what they do for us . . . Dave Evins has been doing things for us for a long time . . . He suggested a pleat for the Dormie scuff . . . It went over well . . . That's what he got paid for . . . the pleat."

The 420,000 square feet of factory are well swept.

"We have only one sweeper to a plant—that tells a story, doesn't it?" he asks wryly.

The factory looks congested, but a second glance reveals there is an orderliness that can come only out of long association. Worker to worker. Management to worker.

Reardon snuffs out the glowing end of his fat 50-cent cigar, removes his suit coat and hangs it on the old, but well kept, wooden coat rack standing in the corner of the small office in Factory No. 2.

"I want them (the employes) to know we're all in this together," he offers in explanation, presuming a shirt-sleeve approach by management establishes greater identity with employes.

He gave a faint tug at the bottom of the dark-blue faint-stripe suit vest that didn't fully conceal his deep blue/gold embroidered suspenders. The tug also called attention to the small diamond-studded pin, given Green employes with 50 years of service, pinned near his lower-left watch pocket.

Some say this snappy septuagenarian is mercurial. More aptly, he is steel on a grinding wheel, showering sparks.

"Our merchandising profit is not high. It is our self-sufficiency that gives me that plus."

He produces a little black notebook and reads. It is one of

two he has. Son John, 43, now executive vice-president who is to succeed his father as soon as a suitable quality-control man with executive talents can be found—carries a copy of ONE notebook. The books have all the facts.

Green makes its own glue and trimmings, does its own fabric combining, makes its own boxes and produces its own electricity, having harnessed with a Reardon-built dam the swift West Canada Creek. What electricity it doesn't use, it sells to the city.

"That creek can really freeze up and flood. One year I used 15,000 pounds of dynamite to set it free. Another year, before the dam went in, it cut the company roads down 17 feet."

He's prideful the factories are heated automatically now. Firetenders need no longer apply, and the space once housing giant boilers now provides additional warehouse space.

"We're approaching electronic data processing, but we're going to creep into it, probably sending it out to a "service station." One of my friends in California has spent an awful lot of money before he got it to working right."

Looking at the old wooden shipping crates, stamped "Daniel Green Felt Shoe Company," nailed one on top of the other to make warehouse shelving, it's hard for the casual observer to believe EDP will ever come to Dolgeville and the 85-year-old Daniel Green Co.

But wait again!

The machinery in the factories . . . The machinery is a United Nations . . . There's a clicker from Italy, a Freeman tack puller ("The first machine I ever ran and still the best tack puller ever made") and machines from Germany, England, France, the U. S.

Then Reardon tells about his frequent trips to Europe, to search out new machinery and equipment. Often he traveled with two other machinery-method-obsessed comrades—Wally McGrath of John E. Lucey Co. and the late Charles Slosberg of Green Shoe Co.

Reardon heaps praise on John Disch—"a mechanical genius"—who in 1919, at the age of 19, revolutionized the slipper industry by designing at Green the first machine to sew a sock lining to a soft sole slipper. He has been with the firm ever since. As a result, overhead wheels whir and cogs mesh in an unrelentingly efficient manner, but with overtones of those early factory scenes at the beginning of the Industrial Revolution.

But there's nothing provincial about Warren Reardon. Both sons—John and Warren, Jr., 41, who is factory superintendent—were sent to European factories to get a worldly view of the shoe business.

"Look at this color—iced plum," the elder Reardon said, picking up a slipper. "Why, I wouldn't be caught dead putting in a number like that. But John did it, and he's probably right for fall . . . I'm a technical man. John is much more well-rounded and I'm glad."

Reardon, Green, Dolgeville, pursuit of better footwear machinery, greater self-sufficiency, all seem to be inseparable. To know president Reardon is to know them all. He epitomizes that Yankee trait called "industry"—an innate desire "to make things go."

It is related to the elder Reardon turning up at 7 a.m. at the plant six days a week. "And after Mass on Sunday," he adds.

However, son John's appraisal differs: "It's not that we like hard work," he smiles. "But there's not much else we have to do around here."

Footwear is Warren Reardon's life, going back to his boyhood at Quincy, Mass., where the odor of leather "tantalized me as I passed the factories on the way to school." It's Reardon, the youth, bucking the idea of entering the family business—a produce brokerage. A lifetime of shoes, starting as a "cripple (defective shoe) boy" at Rice & Hutchins, then a long apprenticeship that led from quality control to Dolgeville and factory management, to the Daniel Green presidency in 1945.

Reardon retired the preferred stock in 1946; split 2 for 1 in 1948, and split 3 for 1 in 1960. The firm is producing more than 2.5 million pairs annually and aims for 3 million by 1970.

"That's capacity for us without adding other buildings," he said. "Beyond 3 million pairs, let the other fellow make them."

An outspoken foe of conveyorization per se, Reardon decries it as "a mechanical pacesetter, which sacrifices quality because workers always wind up chasing it. We do have conveyors but only to move goods swiftly from one location to another. (One unique conveyor application is to roll leather for the clicker operators.)

"Walkin' and talkin' have always been the biggest causes of production lacks. Our clicker operators had this problem. They would walk to the leather cage and pick up the dies and the leather bundle. Now one man selects the dies and rolls each hide individually with a conveyor that drops it into a hand truck. When a clicker operator needs more work, he pushes a button and the work is brought to him. We now save 19–20 per cent in labor costs on this operation alone."

Reflecting perhaps his days as a "cripple boy," the Green operation maintains no repair department.

"Repairers make people killers. Cripples are sent back to

the people who made them and they do them over. And they don't get paid for the time it takes to repair them. They've already been paid once to make them." He spoke with that air of prudent finality that only native New Englanders seem to be able to muster.

He is a light turner-offer. A door-closer to preserve paid-for heat. A man who doesn't ask questions of his employes just to be asking them, as he makes his self-appointed rounds.

He utilizes fabric selvage to bundle slipper components; scraps are often turned into trimming, and he has a welter of Disch-designed "status quo" machines to keep lasts lasting longer—such as the Rube Goldberg-like one with the two shoehorns on a long arm to pull slippers on the last. The old way was to yank them on with a hand tool, which often battered the last's heel and destroyed its true size.

"It's the little things that count. The big things take care of themselves." He was crossing the street in the direction of the main building. "Look at those windows," he said, suddenly pointing.

"I have all those window shades pulled half-way down at quitting time every day. Looks good, but that's not the main reason. Whoever pulls them down will notice if a window is open. Suppose a window was left open and we had a big storm. It could ruin a lot of work."

This urge to get things right has led him in later life toward bank and association directorships. He used to golf and hunt big game, but too many of his friends have died off to make it interesting any more. However, he plans to start golfing again this summer—with his grandson.

His acceptance of directorships in Endicott Johnson Corp. and A. E. Nettleton Co. stem from "obligations of favors" rendered in the past to him. His presence on these boards originally was to protect a widow's inheritance and to ease a tenuous father-son relationship.

Reardon's interest in the National Footwear Manufacturers Association led him to a three-time regional vice-presidency, the chairmanship of the investment committee and a long-time directorship in NFMA, finally resolving itself into a lifetime directorship awarded in 1963.

What about the future—when John takes full command? Will there be a fourth generation of Dolgevillians working at the Daniel Green plant, John prowling the aisles and stopping to ask an operator with 39 years' service whether something new like the American Safety Cable needle spotter, costing Green $175 each, has been able to hike the operator's daily production? ("Yes, it does—three to four more cases per day," one tells the elder Reardon. "Good. Good for you, Mary," replies Reardon. "We want to increase production, but we don't cut the piece rate. That operator gets 3 cents a pair. There's 10 pair per case. That means an extra $1.20 per day," he says.)

"You know, of the 42 executives in the company, I'm the only one who ever worked for another shoe company. We have three generations working for us. We could never duplicate this plant. You can't buy loyalty.

"We never hesitate to bring our competitors here and show them our plant. We worry when they don't copy us. The more they copy us, the closer their prices will be. They can look at our machinery all they want."

(Later, Mr. Reardon reneged on the machinery offer. One machine, which Green developed is definitely out of bounds to competitors—the one that puts a scuff together without putting a tack in the last.)

"I'm not worried about John. He can be very objective.

And don't for one minute believe this is a one-man organization. If I throw something down and walk out one door, he'll be in a few minutes later through the other door and pick up what I threw down."

Son John has already revamped the sales force—many of the elder Reardon's contemporaries having retired. He's hired men from outside the shoe business—for example, a used car salesman and an undertaker. The sales manager, V. P. Robinson, was John's commanding officer in the Marines, a full colonel.

John continues the company policy of direct consumer advertising, with no cooperative allowances, but has added magazines like Ebony to the list. ("Our product is aimed at people of good taste in every income bracket.")

Says John of his father, "We hack at each other like men do . . . I've always loved him, but I've learned to respect him. No father-son relationship can succeed without the element of respect."

CHAPTER 4

Man in Motion

John B.
Reinhart, Jr.

JOHN B. REINHART, JR., in his 24th year as president of infants' shoe manufacturing Trimfoot Co. is a man on whom literary allusions are easily pinned.

Call him a Conradian figure and he'd laugh, despite a

special appetite for Joseph Conrad tales. But it's a good bet
that when the eyelids go heavy at some industry conclave,
the handsome, urbane executive is thinking Conrad
thoughts, sea thoughts.

This side of 56, he resembles one of the Cassini brothers.
His hair is silver at the temples, his build medium and well-
conditioned. His clothes have the classic cut. His shoe wardrobe runs the gamut from sneakers to patent dancing pumps
and 10-inch hunting boots. He flew a multi-engine plane for
14 years, then gave it up because he couldn't convince himself he was professional enough.

He is on first meeting quiet, cool, intense. The body is in
one place, the mind in another. Feet planted solidly on the
ground, thoughts wandering out to sea, the manner always
generous.

Get him a few miles out on a boat, his friends say, and he
opens up: Raconteur par excellence, pleasure-loving deadly
serious sportsman. The contradiction is in character.

He grew up in the Midwest where the rivers run dry, but
he caught salt in his mittens when he was a kid sailing
around Cape Cod and he's never shaken free of it.

He has what the British call "side," an ability to hold part
of himself in reserve, never give himself away completely.
But the tone that comes through most clearly—the confidence, thoughtfulness, clarity and directness—is thoroughly
American.

The genre is "successful American business."

"I'm just a country boy from the gravel switch." The
image is left to float around the room, the speaker retreats
behind a wry but affable smile.

He is complete master of any situation in which he finds
himself. Wherever he is, in a group at an industry meeting
or sitting alone in the lobby of the Waldorf with his own

thoughts, he manages to set up his own field of tension. "It's a matter of fission," an associate says.

It is no coincidence, then, that in a short time he has become a power in the inner circles of the shoe industry. He held the presidency of the National Footwear Manufacturers Association for 1966.

Neither is it coincidence that Trimfoot, reflecting Reinhart's personal traits of excellence, has moved to the front ranks in the children's shoe field.

The sea thoughts are one side of the coin. Trimfoot's drive upward is the other.

"When I came to Trimfoot, annual sales were equal to what is now our monthly breakeven figure.

"Eleven years ago, domestic sales were approximately $5 million. Two years ago they ran substantially in excess of $10 million. In 1966 they gained more than another 10 per cent.

"Sales overseas (United Kingdom and Europe) quadrupled in the past five years. Great potential there for footwear, and we're in with both feet.

"We bought Moran Shoe Co. (Carlyle, Ill., infants' shoe producer). We made the deal to round out our price spread. Our Baby Deer brand covers the $3–$7 price points in the department store field. Moran's Wee Walker line goes to the variety store field at $1–$3.

"We'll do 60 per cent of our business in the two national brands, 40 per cent in private labels at volume.

"But we don't have any other acquisitions in mind now. No more holes to fill at present. We go heaven to seven now. We haven't done all we could in that field. Most anything is possible. But for the moment, we'll stick to our lasts.

"The divisions are run by brand managers who, in turn, answer to a marketing manager and an executive committee.

I put in an 8–6 day, spend one day a week at each of the
plants (Carlyle and Farmington, Mo.), an occasional trip to
the Baby Deer division of Savage, Ltd., in Ontario (a licensing arrangement) rest of the time at headquarters in St. Louis.

"St. Louis is just home. I got into the shoe business there
in 1935 traveling for the Wizardlite Foot Appliance Co.,
after graduating from Washington University and putting in
a stint with Gardner Advertising Co. (on the Ry-Krisp and
Monsanto Chemical accounts). Went with Trimfoot as a
salesman in the late 1930s, moved up to advertising manager, made president in 1946.

"I don't see any merit in the arguments offered by the industry's critics that it's antiquated or protectionist.

"Techniques in marketing and merchandising are more
advanced than they've ever been. I think more objective decisions are being made, based on facts. When everyone finds
what business they're in and works at it, a great period will
be possible.

"We're beginning at last to attract people into the industry
on a parallel with other industries. People with well-rounded
backgrounds with zeal and imagination. At least they're
imaginative enough to see the vacuum in the industry and
the opportunities it presents.

"The legacies are leaving our business. There was a time
when there were buggy whips in the industry. But we turned
that corner five years ago.

"If by protectionist you mean quotas, I think any industry
has the right to insist on antidumping legislation. And I'd
urge every one in the industry to support the Muskie Orderly
Marketing Bill.

"This isn't an easy industry to break into anymore. I don't
know of any time when greater personnel and capital re-
serves have been needed.

"Manufacturers are constantly providing greater service to the vendors. Investment in the business has to take this into account. The whole investment, not just capital, is the most it's ever been.

"There's no getting away from this. Retailers are perhaps more sensitive to the elements necessary for a profitable operation than ever before. Each is finding his own level. It's the beginning, I feel, of a whole new era.

"We are really in the look better, feel better business. It's like the cosmetic business. We're selling hope. I feel we'll tend more toward that in the future. We have to educate the consumer, not only in the health aspects of footwear but appearance, wearing different shoes for different occasions. The population is more mobile than it's ever been. The family is on the go and everyone goes with it. Children go wherever the family goes and they go dressed for the occasion. We're constantly putting footwear on ever-lower age groups. That's a positive trend the industry should get behind, apparel for the occasion.

"I'm two types. Either very casual. Or sort of classic. I believe in wearing clothes for the particular activity or environment.

"I'm a great sportsman, very interested in migratory fowl, hunting, raising Labrador dogs. Spend a good deal of time light-tackle fishing, tagging fish in the Bahamas for the National Oceanographic Foundation.

"I'm aboriginal enough to have to spend a lot of time outdoors and draw refreshment from it to appreciate the vacuums in my business life.

"What you learn from out-of-doors is the ruthless law of nature. Survival of the fittest. I suppose you can apply the lesson to the free enterprise system. On the other hand, nature will teach you to be within keeping of nature's charac-

ter, to be fair. It draws your interest to little things. Makes
you project a social responsibility. Socially conscious and
consumer conscious are the same thing.

"We're selling a product through and not just to the consumer."

"I think this thinking has been evident in actions of the
current Administration. I may not be in accord with the way
some of it has been projected. But I'm in accord with the
basic ideas.

"We all have a lot to learn. I think it's encouraging that,
through the National Footwear Manufacturers Association
conference in Atlantic City, we're attracting more foreign
visitors. We'll all gain from that. But I didn't expect to do
any traveling on the industry's behalf when I was president
of the association. I was no emissary. There was too much
personal business. But I traveled on my own and I'm for it
for everyone in the industry. As the industry becomes exposed to other cultures, as consumers become exposed to
other cultures, I think it will rub off on the kind of materials
we use and wear, in the colors. You can look around and see
evidence of that.

"The possibilities are enormous. I look at the American
market as only 4 hours wide and 3 hours high. That's the
way we should be. And the world market is 12 hours wide
and 6 hours high."

The thought sends his mind wandering again. He drops
behind the eyelids, checks his thoughts, eyes his empty glass.
Time to go.

"No, I wouldn't want to spend all my time out-of-doors.
I'm not completely aboriginal. Just enough. I'd still have to
be around people and products.

"I always knew if I were sensitive to people's needs I
could find an area in which to make a mark. What would I

do if I wasn't in the shoe business? The question reminds me of a fellow I used to fish with. 'Tom,' I once asked him, 'if you had one bait to choose, which would it be?' He said he'd choose a possum-nosed plug. I asked, 'If you had two baits to choose, which would you choose?' He said, 'Two possum-nosed plugs.' "

Part Two

The Wise Capitalists

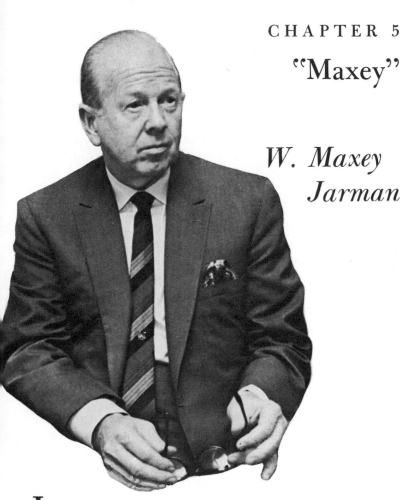

CHAPTER 5

"Maxey"

W. Maxey Jarman

IN THE OFFICE of the head of Genesco, Inc., a circle of
light from a motion picture projector plays on a white wall all
day long. The projector is one of the few continuously projecting kaleidoscopes extant, casting an unending series of
patterns on W. Maxey Jarman's wall.

He showed the contraption to a visitor with relish. "It never repeats a pattern," he noted with satisfaction. "I like toys," he added, exhibiting the kind of boyish enthusiasm that if you have built the largest footwear, apparel and retail complex on the planet, you can well afford to exhibit.

It was an infrequently seen, frivolous side of this deadly serious, highly complex, intensely introspective corporate manager. In 1967, he is 2 years from his mandatory retirement, something of a legend in his own time (certainly the only man in the shoe business instantly identifiable by his given name), the rare example of a man who has successfully made the leap from shoe dog to front rank corporation executive replete with impressive directorship (Federal Reserve Bank of Atlanta, Mutual of New York Insurance Company), knowledgeable public relations counselor and invitations to lunch with the editorial board of The New York Times.

A little thicker in the frame, a little heavier around the jaw than he was when he used to frequent shoe shows, Maxey still comes on powerful, articulate, charming, engaging, vastly sophisticated and equipped with the fastest set of reflexes since Pepper Martin, the legendary St. Louis Cardinals' base-stealer.

Sometimes lolling on his couch, sometimes perching on a teakwood cabinet, Jarman talked about the shoe business corporate management, the clothing business and assorted other subjects, projecting a series of strongly held views, which like his kaleidoscope, never repeated themselves. Thus—:

There's no fundamental difference between running a shoe business and an apparel business. The shoe business tends to be a business that demands a lot of working capital. That's its trouble. It ought to need more fixed assets. That's the real trouble with the shoe manufacturing business. There's not enough investment in plant. We're not going to get that under the present system of multiplicity of styles and frequent style change. I'm not talking about a significantly larger investment in plant. Only a little more fixed capital would be needed, really.

Footwear production is pretty static despite the rise in incomes and the growth in population. I think we don't really know what customers want. We don't put enough emphasis on comfort in shoes. People—particularly men—are buying more casual wear. Yet we think of men's footwear in terms of the traditional laced oxford.

We think too much about price. People have money. You can't make an appeal on low-end merchandise. We ought to get higher prices for shoes and we ought to give better service in our stores.

Footwear people have not done enough toward marketing their product by functional classification. It's a system we're putting in throughout Genesco. We call it Trend Identification. Federated Department Stores calls it Customer Preference. Sears calls it something else. A side effect of the classification is to permit a numbering system that feeds directly into computers.

Most businesses do 75 per cent of their volume on 25 per cent of their products. I've never been able to convince people of that. When we took over Kress—thousands of items —the management didn't believe it. Well, it turned out that Kress did 82 per cent of its business on 25 per cent of its merchandise—soft goods, jewelry, cosmetics.

[Maxey paused to examine his Johnston & Murphy black calf wingtips with woven vamp plug propped up on a low

table. The shoes were laced oxfords. He returned a Genesco
systems manual to its place in a long row of such volumes
that line his office bookcases. He resumed.]

We've had a good year [Sales $760 million; Profit $22.4
million]. Our shoe business is medium profitable. It's our
largest division in sales [39 per cent, or $321,000,000—
more than Brown's, less than International's] but not in
profits. Our best performer in terms of return on capital? Our
outerwear business. We expect to increase our shoe business
profitability dramatically [by intense efforts toward tight inventory and raw material control, one learns from other
sources. Informed guesses put Genesco's footwear earnings
above 2 per cent of sales, but not the best performance in the
industry].

Our I. Miller business is up. I had been making the decisions there myself for many years.

Why hadn't I. Miller been profitable while our Johnston
& Murphy business has been a great success? We bought
them both about the same time, both with serious management deficiencies. I'm not sure of the answer.

There's nothing intrinsically different about the men's or
women's shoe business that would make either one harder
to operate than the other. I think we had more confidence in
our judgment with J & M. We took a strong hand immediately. Management there virtually did not exist. We moved it
to Nashville—everyone said we couldn't maintain quality.
Nonsense. Just the reverse. Our people were so pleased at
working on fine shoes that quality improved. Finally, we had
good management at J & M. When you come down to it, it's
the management that makes the difference in this business.

I. Miller? We were indecisive. We felt we didn't know the
women's high priced fashion shoe business, so we deferred
to the judgment of people we thought knew more about it

than we did. They were wrong—and we were wrong and the thing went from bad to worse. We finally had to move the factory out of New York. I ran things there, so you can see for yourself how well I've done.

Of course we buy companies now in a much different manner and for a different purpose than when we first started building through acquisition. We used to buy bargains. We'd get the tax loss carry forward and all that. No more. We buy sound functioning companies with good management.

What are our criteria? What is our plan for acquisitions? We want companies that lend themselves to large corporate management. Such industries as men's hats, or men's and women's hosiery don't, and we're not interested. We want management. We simply have no plan, as such. We have long range corporate goals, but we don't plan to buy this company or that company. [Genesco didn't plan to buy the Kress variety chain. The deal was dreamed up by a pair of brilliant, imaginative Wall Street bankers who showed Jarman how he could buy Kress, sell off the real estate, and own the whole thing without its costing Genesco a dime.] We might be interested in buying a few more men's wear stores, but that's partly defensive—our competitors are actively buying up retail outlets.

I can't see the discount business. There's no future in it. Korvette tried to lose its discount image. Those leased shoe departments are eventually going to be taken over by the stores. That's been the whole history of the department store business. When a department becomes profitable, the store takes it over.

What we have to offer an acquisition is not a new insight into their industry. No. We offer professional management and continuity of management. We have the art of running a business. Most medium and small businesses do not understand capital and how to use it. Use of capital is central to what we do. Our divisions are required to maintain a standard of profitability, to turn their capital at a stated rate and to achieve a planned return on their capital. The divisions lay out the broad lines of planning and we managers help them reach their sales and profit goals.

The big shoe companies have failed to provide depth in management (so have we in Bonwit's)—U. S. Shoe and Brown would be notable exceptions, but few of the others have really done anything about it. All the news the past few years about shoe companies doing poorly and having management problems haven't enhanced the attractiveness of shoe companies as investments in the eyes of Wall Street.

We try to look ahead. We have a Trend Committee that examines the trends of living. We meet every Wednesday with people from outside our business in a kaffeeklatsch. We are continually reviewing our corporate structure. Cross fertilization of ideas is important. So is communication. The office grapevine is a powerful medium of intra-company communication; we use it all the time.

Business abroad. Maybe. We were approached by French bankers not long ago to organize an apparel business there, but we didn't have the management to spare for such an operation. We don't find any coolness to American investment in Europe, by the way. South America? No. We're cool to South America. Too financially and politically unstable. But we like Mexico. We wouldn't be interested in a Bata-type operation in the low-income nations of Africa and Asia. That's not for us.

When I retire, I'll drop all active participation in Genesco. I'll keep a directorship, but that doesn't mean much. So many directorships mean nothing. I'm a director of the Atlanta

Federal Reserve Bank. They don't pay the slightest attention to my views. I'm on the board of Mutual of New York. The management runs that business. They need prominent citizens on the board, so they picked me. Genesco has often considered outside directors—we have none. But every time we get to considering men, we run into all kinds of problems of who to pick and who to leave off and who we'll offend and who we'll flatter, so we give up the idea.

Retirement? I've got plans, which I'll keep to myself. Hobbies? Mrs. Jarman and I like to travel. I'm a collector— abstract art, eggs (no Fabergé. Too expensive.), elephants. Government service is not for me. I'd hate one of those ceremonial jobs. My job here has a certain amount of ceremony and I'm impatient with it. I'm a man of action.

I like men around me who are realistic. It's a rare quality. I like men who are not afraid to take a position. J. P. Morgan said the most important quality in a businessman is character. I agree with that. The man of highest character won't necessarily be a success in business, but I've found that high character is the common denominator of most successful men I've ever known.

CHAPTER 6

The Medici of Milk Street

E. Morton Jennings, Jr.

"A BUSINESSMAN ought to use as much of his skill and artistry in getting his customers to pay bills promptly as he does in selling his products. A businessman can make more money than you might imagine by getting his customers to pay on time.

"Keep your cash flowing. Turn your capital. What counts is return on capital."

E. Morton Jennings, Jr., senior vice-president of the First National Bank of Boston, ticked off a few cardinal rules for financial health with the subtle blend of earnestness and knowledgeability that is the hallmark of the man accustomed to giving advice tactfully. And having it followed.

He is one of that group of men, a special breed, on whom his fellows have conferred the right to look into the secret places of men's lives.

Physicians and clergymen have it. Psychiatrists and accountants acquire it. Bankers need it.

Mort Jennings, a banker for 40 years, has looked into all the secret places of the vast industry that converts the hides of animals (and, lately, man-made substances) into coverings for the feet.

He believes his bank lends more money to the footwear industry—from hide dealer to retailer and everyone in between—than any other institution in the world, and there is no one to dispute him. Mr. Jennings' job, until he was elevated to the senior vice-presidency last year, involved him directly, as a major area of responsibility, with financing the footwear industry. He has seen more of its secret places than most men.

"More and more shoe men have come to realize the importance of money," he notes, adding: "They don't realize the importance of money until they need it. That's what I mean about working hard to collect your accounts receivable. You should have the money at work for you.

"The trick is to turn your working capital and make it work harder and faster for you. There is considerable talk in the shoe business about profit on sales. That's important. But what really matters is return on capital.

"The way to improve your return on capital is to use it effectively, to turn it as rapidly as possible. A good shoe manufacturer might turn his capital up to 10 times a year. His net on sales would be small, but at the end of the year, he'd have made a fine profit.

"A smart businessman will use borrowed money for leverage. A businessman should cultivate a good relationship with his banker. He should share his problems with his banker. Be close to him. A banker should be accepted as an adviser—in many areas. A banker sees many industries, many men, many situations. He has a lot of other people's experiences to draw from. All of it useful to a shoe man. He can help a shoe man defend himself against the unknown.

"I can't count the number of shoe companies—all kinds, tanners, components makers, shoe manufacturers, retailers— who've grown through borrowed money. They grew by expanding their inventories and product lines. They grew through acquiring other companies.

"A banker can relate to all industries. He can lend perspective through his contacts outside a narrow field. That's our stock in trade. I couldn't possibly tell a man how to run a shoe business."

A telephone call for Mr. Jennings (a department store chain needs a few million dollars on a seasonal basis) and his visitor surveys the splendidly spacious room in which the banker works.

It is magnificent. Tan stone soars to a vaulted gilt ceiling, a luxurious contrast to the massive bland exterior of hewn stone in the Florentine style. A Medici palace on Milk Street, Boston. Mr. Jennings' desk at the end of the room is approached through ranks of subordinate vice-presidents. Behind his swivel chair is a mural of noble proportions, perhaps 25 feet high. It includes a map of the Western Hemisphere, the sea god Poseidon and Spanish galleons. The artist was Nathaniel C. Wyeth, progenitor of the great Wyeth house of painters. High on his scaffold, a latter day Michelangelo, N. C. Wyeth, wrought in 1923 a monument for the Back Bay Lorenzo the Magnificent who commissioned him.

"We'll go along with what that fellow wants (the big retailer). Big businesses are basically similar to one another whatever the type of industry, so you can size up the problems very quickly. But small businesses are the ones that vary widely, one from the other, industry to industry.

"You're darn right the small shoe business is different from any other business."

Your career has spanned two generations of New England shoe men—the older group that dates from the 1920s and 1930s, tough, fierce competitors, unpolished, immigrants and their sons and sons-in-law, worldly, well-tailored, with Harvard and Dartmouth degrees. What are the chief characteristics of the two groups?

"Ah, yes. The old school. They were artists, in a sense. They had great style ability. They had a wonderful insight into their markets. They operated by feel, by the seat of their pants, you might say. They were plungers and gamblers.

"They gambled most of all on leather. A man would go out and sell his production for the season. Then he'd try to figure out how he would make the shoes at a profit.

"He'd do it chiefly by gambling with leather. He'd try to buy leather at a penny under the market, buy for his entire season. If he could swing it, he'd have a successful season; if he couldn't, he'd have a loss—maybe go under.

"They're still gambling with leather on Lincoln and South Streets [the footwear manufacturing and leather districts], but they're getting away from it.

"The older generation often didn't know its true costs. As I say, there was a lot of intuitive business done.

"The younger men are different. They are extremely cost-conscious. They know what a shoe costs before they make it, or they figure the costs before they make a commitment. That's one of the chief differences between the generations.

"They're getting away from gambling on leather and averaging the costs of leather out over the season. Of course, the introduction of LIFO smoothed out leather prices. The new generation wants to make a manufacturing profit, not a leather profit.

"The younger men are more deliberate in analyzing their markets and studying their operations objectively—you have to, for instance, if you want to use a computer.

"The older men lived by their wits, by their latent merchandising and style abilities.

"A major change in New England (we've been talking about New England, but I want to note that we finance footwear companies all over this country), of course, was the United Shoe Machinery decision which required shoe machinery to be offered for sale. That's a major difference among the generations, although it's one that happened as an outside force.

"In the old days, there were few fixed assets in a shoe factory and this encouraged banks to lend money because the manufacture-capital was highly liquid. But once you bolt the assets to the floor, you've got quite a different picture from a banker's point of view."

Mr. Jennings has a somewhat different new generation problem in his own family. His older son, a Dartmouth man —where Mr. Jennings was Class of 1928—has passed up banking for training to become a computer specialist with a blue chip firm of accountants. "The Citibank of New York

wanted him. He can't work here. The bank won't hire relatives. No nepotism allowed." A second son is a student at
Duke University.

"There's a growing trend to more efficient management
than in the old days. You don't find companies operating at a
loss as you used to.

"Whether the young generation, at bottom, are better
businessmen than their fathers is not yet proven. Few of the
young guys have really made it on their own.

"We watch them closely. We used to think that so-and-
so's son really didn't have the stuff, that he wouldn't cut the
mustard. Well, the boy—he's close to 40—is making it very
nicely. We're watching another young man closely. I had
my doubts about him, but he's beginning to look more
promising to me. There are dozens like him. We watch them,
study them, make up our minds."

*Why haven't New England companies been as active in
the merger trend as companies elsewhere?*

"We've had a few mergers here. But the premise of the
question is right. You've got a lot of very strong-willed, individualistic men here who would not work well with other
men. And they know it.

"For years there has been talk of putting together a big
combine of four or five of the largest companies. But you'd
end up with a Mexican army. Everybody a general. No
privates.

"Many people have the merger fever. They come to me
to talk about it, and I have one question: How would the
deal fit your 'plan on the wall'?

"By that I mean a company ought to have a plan for its
future—where it's going and how it proposes to get there. It
should be purposeful, with a definite goal. Not a haphazard

thing with growth just for its own sake. A company that wants to grow should have it carefully thought out. It should have a plan on the wall.

"What you buy, in the last analysis is management. Nothing is any better than its management.

"For a banker the personal character of the business is more important than the collateral. We've ridden a long time with people we trust and respect.

"Anybody who wants to borrow money has to pass the test of integrity. We've dropped some customers—well rated ones, too—who weren't truthful with us on some particular. I agree with J. P. Morgan who said he wouldn't lend money on all the bonds in Christendom to men he didn't trust. Life's too short to fool with people you don't trust in this business."

As a banker, how do you view the current state of business —particularly shoe business.

"Shoe business is in the best financial shape it has been in for some time.

"But the time will come when a businessman will have to scratch for business. Hell, no, I don't believe the business cycle has been eliminated.

"There are not many people around who remember how it is not to be able to sell your product. A businessman should not overextend himself. He shouldn't go for that last dollar of sales and profit. He shouldn't be greedy."

Part Three

Targeting the Market

CHAPTER 7

Mr. Hush Puppies

Adolph K. Krause

ADOLPH K. KRAUSE has grown with his company.

Just as one can read of the metamorphosis at Wolverine World Wide, Inc. in its financial record, one can spend a few hours with its 65-year-old president and chief executive officer and sense the changes that must have occurred . . .

part businessman, part country boy turned professional corporate manager . . . the engineering grad who went into the
family's small shoe and leather business and engineered a
successful drive to the top with dispatch equaled only by
Clay when he did-in Liston.

A. K. Krause doesn't come on strong—right away. One's
immediate impression is of the quiet, grainy voice, the grey
hair and bespectacled face set on a short, stout, frame . . .
pipe clenched firmly in teeth and, with a few props, the man
would fit equally well as a country doctor or a department
store salesman.

He settles in his chair, props his feet on a hassock and the
interview begins. He switches from pipe to cigar. [He smokes
everything. "I can taste cigarets only in the morning . . .
have two every day before breakfast."] Now he's the corporate executive . . . the voice has a Midwestern accent and
rings of the country . . . he talks of his company and what
has been built . . . he speaks proudly, possessively.

And pride is the proper emotion when you've been the
innovator . . . first to fill a long-known void with a good
product, known and sold by its catchy American name in
17 foreign countries . . . when you've piloted a closely-held
family business around the shoals to a position of leadership
in the American footwear industry, converting it at the same
time into a large, publicly-owned professionally managed
corporation.

Hush Puppies is almost a definition of casuals in itself. It
started the boom . . . It showed everyone "Where it's at." It's
the only footwear made for all members of a family that sells
under a single brand name. Its brushed pigskin look has been
and continues to be copied . . . it is THE prototype casual.

And the way it all happened reads like a business fairy-
tale, complete with happy ending-in-the-black. It's the story

of a company faced with a declining supply of its prime raw material, undecided and indecisive about which turn to take . . . of a machine . . . of shoe industry pioneering in market analysis. Krause talks about it.

"We were basically a work, service and semi-dress shoe company. We started early in the century with horsehide . . . found a way to make it soft without losing its toughness. But the horse population in this country has dwindled from more than 30 million to fewer than 3 million with the coming of the automobile age, so we had to find a new raw material . . . cowhide, which everyone else was using, didn't appeal to us for a variety of reasons.

"When World War II came along the Government asked the help of the meat packers in developing pigskin as a new source of leather, and we were asked to make work shoes out of the skins. The leather was soft and long-wearing but needed a lot of work before it would be suitable for a peace-time consumer market. After the war we bought several of Swift & Co.'s mechanical pig-belly skinners and through our own research, developed a machine that would skin half a hog. That brings us to the mid-1950s."

[This was a major breakthrough in developing pigskin as a feasible shoe material. The skin resembles that of an apple, clinging to the flesh, while cowhide peels like a banana. Formerly, pigskinning by hand was slow and costly, and often damaged the leather. Wolverine is today perfecting a double pig skinner to skin both sides of a hog, giving larger skins for new products and providing cutting economies.]

"In analyzing markets at that time we saw a great potential in leisure shoes. I knew we weren't dress shoemakers and light, comfortable shoes were selling well . . . especially sneakers. So we decided to go after that market. The first shoe was a sneaker pattern with a crepe sole.

"The name came into being at the suggestion of our sales manager. The story goes that he saw some people down south eating corn fritters and tossing some to their barking dogs with the plea to 'Hush, puppies.' We thought it would be catchy to have Hush Puppies to quiet the other kind of barking dogs.

"We had seven names from which we were to choose, and we took a consumer survey to see which would get best acceptance. Hush Puppies came in seventh. But our dealers liked the name and I stuck my neck out and stayed with it . . . lucky guess.

"So in late 1957 we test-marketed 30,000 pairs that we had made for us outside and we found the product marketable. In 1958 we started making only men's in a small room, about 900 pairs daily." [Wolverine's daily output of Hush Puppies stands at about 50,000 pairs today.]

"By mid-1958 we got so far behind with so many orders that we had to turn our semi-dress shoe factory into Hush Puppies production. (We had been trying, not too profitably at the time, to break into the work and semi-dress shoe fields.) And business has just gone straight up since then just as fast as we could build factories and get leather."

And that it has. Annual sales that first year were $11.3 million. Seven years later, in 1965, they were $55.4 million.

Earnings the year of the big breakthrough were $322,000. In 1965 they were up 12.8 per cent to $4.8 million.

Per share earnings tell a story: From 27 cents in 1958 to $1.85 in 1966, with stops along the way for a 2-for-1 split in 1959, a ten per cent stock dividend in 1961, a 2-for-1 split in 1962, a 5-for-4 split in 1964 and another 2-for-1 split in 1966. Cash dividends zoomed from 9 cents in 1958 to 40 cents in 1965 on the many times split stock.

"Return on invested capital can be overemphasized. Net

per dollar sale is a more meaningful figure because one can get into shoe manufacturing with a relatively small capital investment. Last year our return on capital invested was 27.8 per cent. But that's nothing to brag about . . . it indicates we can't keep up with our growth. I wouldn't want it under those conditions. The figure wouldn't be so good if we were expanding and servicing as we should have been. We under-planned consistently . . . never planned enough expansion to meet the market's potential. How do you anticipate going from $11 million to $70 million in 8 years? But we've got commitments for $10 million during the next 3 years for plant expansion."

And expansion continues apace. Two major projects are current—a new pigskin tannery, largely automated, in Iowa and a new central warehouse is slated for the firm's head-quarters in Rockford, Michigan, which will have the latest electronic data processing equipment.

A quick walking tour through the new Rockford factory gives one who has even a cursory familiarity with shoe pro-duction lines a sense of being projected into the future. Transporters automatically speed work along modern con-veyor belts to and from operators . . . new machines cut hand operations in the heavier work . . . an intricate roller-bearing conveyor system speeds operations in the packing room . . . all spread out over an enormous but compact area on one level.

Wolverine's success is in some measure due to the unusu-ally large proportion of revenues spent on advertising, and to its methods of determining where to spend that money. If any shoe company could be called market-oriented, could be said to have a marketing approach to selling, Wolverine is it.

"Our advertising is budgeted at 7 per cent of estimated

net sales. Our yearly figure is usually between 6 and 7 per cent." [The average for the shoe industry is about 1½ per cent.] "We use market research to define the areas in which we should concentrate our advertising efforts. (Our average market family has an income of well over $10,000—a good many Hush Puppies are bought as extras.) The media we adopt uses the market as a target. Then all we have to do is find the seasons in which the shoes are usually bought and concentrate the advertising in these periods.

"We've poured lots of money into advertising, and in that regard I think we've made substantial contributions to the shoe industry. We were the first to show our shoes in action, on feet, and that idea has caught on with a lot of others now. But we've always been careful not to show too much of the background, so that virtually anyone can picture himself in the shoes in that setting. In other words, we haven't wanted to 'type' the shoes to a particular income level, kind of person or place. We simply try to show the shoes in highly average situations."

But how did Hush Puppies fill a void in a wide-open market? Why didn't anyone else see it? And how does a company, unsure of where it's going, recognize the holes in the market?

Krause smiles and starts to explain. He sees the answer through a unique pair of glasses.

"We recognized the void when people went canvas. But I'm not so sure it was all a void. I think we created a demand also. Sure, a void was there but we helped establish the nature of the market by creating the type of demand to fill that void. Here's what I mean . . . we didn't have to have brushed pig, crepe-soled shoes—we could have had lightweight welts or slipons instead. Today the void isn't as great, but we've established a generic type to fill what's left. The cool, comfortable, lightweight shoe is still what we swear by."

That cool shoe made Wolverine grow so fast that staff requirements couldn't be filled from within the organization. Having gone outside the company for the first time in 1955 for its board of directors, it again was faced with complex corporate decisions—this time not about products or marketing but about management. Krause tells it the way it happened—disputes among directors, getting an outside board, securing top corporate management as each period's figures topped the last and the company was literally splitting its seams with its own growth.

"We're professional management. Some professional managers are in the family and some aren't. Outside experience has enriched our blend of management. It could be that our attitudes toward managing and growth are different from those of other companies in the industry. But you have to remember that we started as a small, closely-held company, and you might say that all of us have grown as the firm has grown.

"Wolverine is a team effort. As I said, I came up through manufacturing and knew nothing about merchandising—I just guessed. But I've learned a lot about it, and I wasn't interested really. I had a production point of view, but I learned and relied on professional management advice to guide my decisions. My merchandising background comes from experience and working at my job. I'll take credit only for picking good men to do the job. We were able to be successful because of people who started as individuals on a job and took on added responsibility and gained valuable experience as their jobs and departments grew.

"When you grow especially fast, of course, you need more

and more people . . . outside ideas and thinking and experience to go with what you have developed inside the company. Back in 1955 when we were still closely-held, and the supply of horsehide was going down while the price was going up, we needed to decide what our future course would be. Well, there was a real divergence of ideas among the directors about just what direction we should take.

"So for the first time we turned to directors from outside the company to help us plot our course. It was one of the wisest things we've done. They helped us more clearly define lines of authority, helped us evaluate courses of action. This new insight into management, along with the machines, production capabilities and marketing orientation, got us on the right road.

"When we decided to move into foreign markets, we realized the know-how to manage the new international operations would have to come from outside. So we got Austen Wood." [J. Austen Wood is Wolverine vice-president in charge of international operations.] "He had wide experience in foreign markets and fit our needs. Today our foreign licensees are approaching our volume in pairs sold.

"In the past year we hired Lou Schaefer as executive vice-president and elected him a director." [Louis J. Schaefer's strong sales and marketing background is well-known in the shoe industry. His last affiliation was a long one with Brown Shoe Co., where he had been vice-president of sales, a director, executive vice-president and member of the executive committee.] "Lou has more than 30 years of experience in the shoe industry and helps us fill a gap between senior and younger management.

"We thought his background was quite an asset. With our system of district sales managers, our sales director has an administrative job. A man with a marketing background who was a good administrator was what we needed.

"Addition of these men doesn't mean we don't have capable people within the company. It just means that with the kind of growth we're experiencing we feel it's essential to avail ourselves of talent from outside the company, too.

"My philosophy is that everything depends on people. You can research markets, build the right shoes and do everything else right, but it all depends on people. What else is there besides people, basically? If all, I mean all, your people are informed and have incentive and each has a responsibility, then you have a working organization. In our plant each man is a manager, even if he's got nothing more to manage than his own job.

"The success of any business is people. The choice of people, their training and coordinating, motivating them—I think these are about 90 per cent of a manager's job. The rest is checking on results and planning for the future.

"The ideas that adapt raw material to product to market all are the result of the work and thinking of people. I talk with our people about the things of interest and importance to them in our operation—I probably spend as much time at the desks of others as I do at my own. Give a fellow a chance to talk in his own office and he relaxes . . . talks more freely about things he might not even bother to tell me if he came to my office.

"Of course there isn't time to talk with everyone every day—and I shouldn't have to. When a business grows as ours has in a relatively few years, you have to manage by exception—don't worry about what is going well, concentrate where there are problems.

"When we first started, marketing was most important and

that took a lot of my attention. Three and four years ago we
were concentrating on setting up foreign licensees—drawing
up agreements, finding the companies we wanted to make
and sell the shoes in other countries. After that we spent a
lot of time working with production people on ways to build
up our capacity. Last year we were faced with the problem
of developing more interest among packers for our pigskin
procurement program—I found out more about that end of
the business than I ever knew before.

"No one can give everything all his attention constantly.
That's why we have people responsible for certain jobs.
When something special is needed in those jobs, we try to
work more closely with them.

"The right people in the right jobs devoting the right
thinking and energies gives a team real confidence and enthusiasm. At least it has with us. And something else important. There must be motivation if the right people are to do
the right jobs right. Dollar incentive is the common denominator of motivation in everyone, but only up to a point. Motivation is more than dollars—it's building pride of accom-
plishment, appealing to personal pride, giving the person
authority commensurate with his responsibility.

"What it amounts to is that we have personalized company goals so every person has incentive to do a better job.
Then a person takes a different attitude toward his work. We
started this in 1957 when we had that 30,000-pair trial run.
We put a plan into effect that gives employes a way to profit
directly from their own efforts. Employes work as units but
the contributions any individual may make in saving time or
money provide increased earnings for the entire unit. The
plan slogan is 'Work smarter, not harder,' and it's to promote use of head as well as hands.

"Our people are encouraged this way to find ways to do

their jobs in less time, to eliminate rework by doing it right the first time, to stop delays and waste through suggestions for improved processes or techniques, to spot uses for new materials, to handle equipment and material with care, to be on the job regularly and on time.

"These all contribute to the basic cost of a work unit's job, whether it's in production, sales or general office work. Now who's in the best position to help reduce the basic costs, to improve the way a job is being done? The person doing the job, naturally. Give him the financial incentive to do the job better and the responsibility to think and act and produce and the added pride of accomplishing something for himself, his work unit and his company, and there's motivation at every level."

And what of the future? Where is Wolverine headed? The company is planning for more growth and expansion and has assembled one of the most sophisticated professional management teams in the shoe industry to take it wherever it's going. Which roads will it take?

Krause rolls his cigar between his fingers . . . his expression changes . . . brow furrows . . . a long pause for thought.

"I can't in my own mind see why there should be any limit to Wolverine's growth as a corporation. It may or may not take a turn toward more diversification. We've looked at several companies but haven't found any to be compatible with our merchandising. With all the growth in our own endeavors and possibilities in our raw material, we really haven't given much thought to diversification."

[Beside making Hush Puppies, Wolverine makes gloves, hats, ski boots and pole carriers and is making a strong bid in the service shoe market with increased emphasis on its Wolverine brand.]

"We're not against diversification but it's got to be awfully attractive—financially and in terms of manpower. Unless we find something really good, with top management that won't dilute ours, we won't be interested. We have enough potential expansion with our own raw material—and a company without good management would give us problems keeping up with our own needs."

CHAPTER 8

Corfam:
Overture and Act I

William D.
Lawson

"**S**ERENDIPITY," he said. "That's what our penetration of the market was. We overestimated the viscosity of the industry in accepting Corfam."

Serendipity. Viscosity. The jargon of the chemist meets

the insider lingo of the wide-ranging corporate executive of the 1960s.

Not the kind of language one might expect to hear from a man striving to penetrate the hurly-burly footwear industry with a new product.

But it is the language of Du Pont's man for Corfam—precise, serious, open, humorous with the wryness of a man who sees, clear-eyed, his own role in Du Pont's strategy to become a major factor in the footwear business, Du Pont's role in the economic scheme of things, the footwear industry's role as the object of their affection and the fact that the name of the game is profits.

Du Pont's man is William D. Lawson, and he bears the title of manager of the Poromeric Products division. If you know nothing about Bill Lawson, not even his name, you would know instinctively that Du Pont, having expended uncounted millions in developing Corfam, would scan its voluminous roster of rising executives with extreme care and selectivity to choose the man to watch over and guide this huge investment. Out of this rigorous corporate selection process has emerged Bill Lawson.

He discourses on Corfam:

"Our curve of sales penetration is a little better than we had originally predicted. Our marketing manager, Charlie Lynch, did a magnificent marketing job.

"The introductory expenses were high—higher than we'd expected for the research and production problems. Our management efficiency is constantly improving. But marketing expenses were in line with forecasts.

"But we made mistakes. First we overestimated the viscosity of the industry in accepting Corfam. So a good part of our Corfam sales was serendipity as far as our program was concerned.

"A larger error was in underestimating the lead time we'd taken to bring Corfam on stream in Old Hickory, Tenn. We estimated 9 to 18 months and it took all of that and more. The manufacture of Corfam is a very disciplined operation involving complex chemical engineering. Temperature control is crucial and must be absolute. It can take as long as 5 years to get a process like Corfam into full production. It won't take us that long. But it is taking longer than wishful thinking might have indicated.

"Corfam is hard to make. There's a false notion that Corfam is a cheap product selling at a high price. Actually, it's the other way around. It's an expensive product. The price of Corfam at its introduction was a subsidy. Now, the price is at a transition stage relative to our costs.

"Sure. The price of Corfam will decline gradually as our market expands. We want a good share of the market. The bigger the share, the larger the profit. I won't disclose what share we're aiming at, but we are a little more optimistic than we used to be about the share of the market we can get at any given price level."

Lawson rises to fetch a book. His shoulder brushes a group of framed photographs of B-17s wheeling in the sky. Lawson was a bomber pilot in World War II and emerged a much-decorated Major. Another photograph is an aerial color shot of the Corfam plant. He returns with a thick loose-leaved book, titled "Corfam Venture Analysis."

"All our studies are in this book—studies of every possible variable that might affect the market for Corfam. Cattle population, feed prices, human population, worldwide growth, income and spending patterns, shoe worker wages— everything conceivable bearing on our product. We are continually updating the studies. To resolve these studies rapidly into a set of answers is beyond even the powers of

Du Pont's elaborate computers setup. We have to rent time on outside computer equipment, one that the Department of Defense also uses.

"Our studies show there'll be a long range population growth accompanied by shortages in raw materials. We'll be competing for this increment in the market for non-leather material as other manufacturers of upper materials enter the market.

"I'm sure we'll have strong competition, even though we've built a good patent complex—we've patented a chemical structure, not footwear upper material.

"It's going to take very sophisticated chemistry to compete against us. The kettle-and-paddle type of chemical manufacturer is not going to make it, in my judgment. Some have even dropped out of this effort. I'd guess the skillful chemical companies such as Union Carbide or Imperial Chemicals and Carl Fruedenberg, abroad, have the skills to bring out a competitive product.

"We've seen many products. Many are permeable. Permeability is easy to achieve. There are many more qualities that go into Corfam that haven't yet been duplicated.

"Licensing? There's no thought of that now.

"It's possible our future role as a supplier to footwear manufacturers will simply be as a producer of Corfam 'gray goods.' Our arrangements with Fleming Joffe and Allied Kid might lead you to suspect that. Actually, we want their fashion expertise and their feel for the shoe business. They both specialize in new colors and finishes. We'll continue to make finished Corfam, with a tendency for us to concentrate on the basic colors and effects.

"We want to make a better product; to make one that's easily and profitably usable by our customers. That's not altruism. That's plain, good business.

"All experience shows that a higher percentage of consumer spending goes into a product if it is better in terms of the consumer's perceived value. So, the way to get people to spend more for a product is to improve it. This is what will increase per capita consumption of footwear."

Lawson leads his visitors to lunch through the rabbit-warren maze of corridors that Du Pont tucks many of its Wilmington operations into. He is a lean, trim, tweedy 49 years old. He lopes down the corridors with the long stride of a 6-foot-twoer, his body stooped forward in an attitude suggestive of a ski-jumper at the takeoff moment.

He chats about his children—two boys and a girl. The eldest, a boy, "might make a fine physicist some day." The boy's father holds a chemical engineering degree from Cornell, and he misses the lab, now that he is a management man.

He started out with Du Pont in 1949 as a chemist and began his ascent of the corporate pyramid almost immediately, moving through positions of increasing responsibility to his present level in 1962.

"I like to fool with small-capacity racing autos. But not to race them. Once, I dickered a long time for a Ferrari." He smiles modestly at the audacity of owning a Ferrari. "I'm a passionate trout fisherman. My favorite spot is in the Laurentians of Quebec. I take my wife along. It's wild country."

Luncheon in the stately, paneled Du Pont dining room. A round of Bloody Marys; the season's first shad, perfectly grilled; fresh crab with the tang of Carolina shoal water still on it. An excellent lunch. The conversation flows on.

"Our two-pronged promotion approach will continue," Lawson says. "Fashion and utility. We intend to emphasize the high price shoe market."

"We're still working on making the material suitable for the tough, bike-braking abrasion-resistance necessary for children's footwear. We're running sales trials right now, and might even introduce it this year. We'll introduce it at the top of the children's price level."

> *Were you dismayed when retailers brought out Corfam shoes under $10?*

Lawson answers carefully: "We think people ought to be realistic about pricing Corfam. It ought to be offered on a sound economic basis and return a profit. I don't know whether those chains were loss-leadering Corfam. A product does best when its customers make money.

"Generally speaking Corfam will find its place in the market where its physical and esthetic properties are wanted. There'll always be acceptance for leather.

"It's possible that one day Corfam will get the kind of acceptance nylon eventually got. I don't know whether Corfam will expand the market for shoes the way nylon expanded the market for hosiery. That took quite a while to come about."

> *You've seen other industries at work, what's your opinion of the footwear manufacturing industry—its sophistication and progressiveness?*

"I think the industry sells itself too short. I'm very familiar with other industries that are like the footwear industry in total volume of sales, number of companies, relative share of the market held by the largest firms, and so forth. Well, the shoe industry is smarter and more progressive in its marketing, technology and product development techniques."

Are there qualities in the footwear industry you think a complex industrial enterprise like Du Pont should have— and vice versa?

"Oh, yes. I admire the way footwear management finds simple solutions to hard problems. Shoemen are quick to decide and quick to act or react. They believe in the rightness of a decision once it is reached and they don't stop to look back.

"On the other hand, I think the footwear industry would do well to pay more attention to management techniques and in building management. Shoe companies lack an orderly structure. There is need for more professional management. Provision should be made for management succession and a better environment created for young people."

CHAPTER 9

Number One

Morton R. Izen

T HE GOOD PEOPLE of Glencoe, Ill., an affluent suburb
of Chicago, find little remarkable in their friend and neighbor
Mort R. Izen. They see little of him, usually on weekends
when he manifests himself rather late in the day, in some

rumpled, knock-about-the-yard outfit, a stubble of beard darkening his jaw and a Corona clenched in his teeth. If the weather is fine he may struggle with his lawn and garden. Or he may simply mooch around the premises.

Early risers in Glencoe during the week may see him headed for his commuter train, neatly dressed in a dark suit, a moderately tall man whose thick chest, and heavy chin give him a slightly foreshortened look. He wears a slightly preoccupied countenance. Sometimes, he appears vaguely annoyed. When he smiles, it is big and warm, and it transforms his face. In short, an American business executive on his way to the office and the battles of the coming day. Nothing remarkable. In Glencoe or anywhere else in the United States.

Nothing remarkable, but for the fact that in a basic world industry he occupies roughly, the position Everest holds among hills.

He is the top. He is Mort R. Izen, supervisor of shoes for Sears, Roebuck, and he puts more shoes on humans' feet than any man on the planet. He is the largest retailer of footwear in the world.

His power is exercised from a large square room in one of Sears' enormous complex of headquarters buildings in Chicago. To reach it, a visitor threads his way through the spare, no-nonsense loft space, partitioned off by buyers' offices and other departments ancillary to the great business of shodding the American public.

At the end of the near-labyrinthine series of corridors, (one not so much visits Sears as makes an odyssey) is Izen's office.

Modishly equipped with contemporary furniture upholstered in bright colors, its walls hung with lively prints of shoes and the shoemaking art, it forms a sharp and handsome contrast with Sears' stark functionalism that lies just outside the office door.

"We are in business to serve the broad middle market of the United States," Mort Izen was saying. "It is a middle market in all respects. Middle in price. Middle in fashion. Middle in sizes. It is THE market.

"It is a market only partially influenced by income. People buy up and out of their economic class. That is central to footwear merchandising, for with people of middle and lower income, shoes come first.

"People want middle fashion. They wear middle sizes. Their preferences have nothing to do with income. Middle sizes, for instance are an integral part of our merchandising program. These sizes constitute 85 per cent of the available market—a market constantly changing in the physical make-up of the people who comprise it.

"The most accurate way I know of to keep track of the changing preferences of this market is through catalog selling. It's a major part of our business and it is the only purely scientific method of evaluating a retailer's selling operation.

"Why? Because everything is recorded. Size, color, style, everything. And what's of great importance, the lost sale is also recorded, for when a customer sends in his money for a specific style in specific color and a specific size, that is it. You can't switch him, you can't fit him to a different size. All you can do is offer him his money back.

"The only thing you can't determine is color preference. If you didn't stock yellow, you'll never know how you might have done with yellow.

"Middle fashion? I call middle fashion the design, or silhouette that is most popular, the one most in demand, the one that people want to buy.

"The pointed toe out of fashion? Not with Sears' customers. The pointed toe is still in fashion and if you walk down the street of this country that's the toe you'll see on women's feet.

"It is the customer who decides this, not Sears. Our motto is simply: 'Let the customer decide.' We listen closely to what the customers are telling us and we listen far in advance—Christmas orders, for example, were all complete by May 20.

"Middle prices? Middle prices are not based on income, or on income statistics, or anything like that. Middle prices are based on what people can afford and are willing to pay.

"We continually test and prod the middle price. We are always trying to raise the level of our transactions. Let's say a men's casual does well at $6. We see what we can add to it in the way of material, or lining or decoration to move the shoe into the $7 category. We don't raise the price, you understand. We offer a better product and we get the higher price for the better product. Then $7 becomes the middle price for that shoe.

"Typically, we'll have a shoe in that category at $8 and one at $6, but $7 will be the volume figure and the middle price.

"Next season, we'll prod and test some more and maybe upgrade that shoe to $8, making that figure the new middle price.

"We ignore all low price business. We ignore discounters. We ignore the bottom of the line in any category.

"By emphasizing upgrading, we increase our profit. And Sears is a profit-minded company. I am expected to show a higher rate of earnings on sales than the footwear industry averages.

"We aim for a repeat business. It's the only business worth

having. The cost of getting the customer the first time makes it unprofitable unless he comes back.

"You must select your market. You cannot be all things to all people. Statistics can tell you only what share of the market you can get. The rest is up to you.

"There is a rising level of taste in this country and desire for better quality merchandise. This trend is not only growing, its growth is accelerating.

"I do not think other shoe retailers understand this concept. I don't want to appear to criticize other shoe retailers, but too many are still behind their market.

"They are doing what I call Shinto merchandising. It's a form of ancestor worship. They're doing what their fathers did and they're falling behind."

Izen veered to a slightly different tack as he expanded on his ideas on upgrading.

"I'm interested in improving the quality of footwear—particularly Sears. We test extensively. In an orphanage, for children's footwear; among our own staff; in men's and women's shoes.

"We have been inspecting our footwear in each of our supplier's plants. Spot check right there before it goes to the stores. Now, we're starting a new program of quality control built around the idea that the manufacturer should see his product the way the consumer sees it."

What about the other end of the pipeline from manufacturer to consumer—the salesclerk?

"We are constantly training our salespeople. We try to give them quick facts on new shoes. We train them in the field by talking to all levels of retail shoe selling.

"But selling shoes is a transitory job. You can't look for permanence in a sales force. Everything is predicated on that.

The average salesman is looking for a better job in the company, or he's putting himself through college, or something like that.

"You can sell shoes without people of course. Self-service? Listen. Sears was the original self-service. We sold through a piece of paper, a picture in a catalog. You can't get more self-service than that."

Sears is renowned for its intimate working relationships with its resources. What are your requirements?

"We like to take 25–35 per cent of a company's output. We take up to 100 per cent with some firms, but those are old resources, and we wouldn't take that much now.

"The resource should be alert to the technological changes going on. In the past we've encouraged innovations such as nylon thread, and cooled needles.

"We ask our resources to establish a statistical control over returns. We watch for foolish economies that are expensive in the long run—like buckles that cost a fraction of a penny a pair less, but which rusted and cost thousands of dollars in returns and customer dissatisfaction.

"We've found it easier to limit our resources. We get 60 per cent of our needs from 10 resources. There's little turnover. Maybe one manufacturer a year doesn't see it our way and is dropped, and a new company comes in.

"We're an important customer wherever we buy. No merger involving a resource has ever taken place without our knowledge. Genesco, for example, has an entire company set up for the sole purpose of supplying our needs.

"We do not 'order' in the normal sense. We have longstanding contractual relationships in which specifications of the product are precisely detailed. We do not write sizes. Our resources know our size needs.

"Our resources stock for us and drop ship to the more than 500 Sears stores that carry shoes. We pay for this inventory. We pay the costs of storage, even the interest on the money. For the true saving is in the logistics of moving shoes.

"Why ship twice? Once to a warehouse, then once again to the store? We reduce the handling by a half. The true saving is in getting the shoes to the right place at the right time.

"Many retailers do not understand this. They continue to complicate the flow from producer to customer by using warehouses. Why? Shinto merchandising. That's the way they've always done it, so they continue to do it that way.

"I think the technological advances in manufacturing have brought benefits. But many of the new materials have more manufacturing benefits than consumer benefits. The synthetic upper materials have yet to bring any great consumer benefits.

"We've had a fine substitute for leather around for some time. Very successful item. It's called canvas."

You are head of the largest retail shoe business in the country and you were also chairman in 1966 of the National Shoe Institute. What is lacking in NSI? What are its potentials?

"There's a great power inherent in NSI. It could be the great educational force in our industry, educating both the industry and the consumer. But we need greater participation of individuals. We need their participation financially and personally. We have the power to build a great force for progress in the footwear industry through NSI.

"We could educate the public in fashion and quality, and in the proper shoe for the proper occasion.

"We have it within our power to educate young people in the bright future of our industry. We could organize a mar-

ket research organization and a product research organization like the British SATRA. We could build a strong core
that our industry lacks. We can build a great future for our
industry.

"But we need people and money. We need a full-time staff
to handle the kind of organization NSI can become. I and
my vice-chairmen, Joe Shell [Shellbro, Yonkers, N. Y.],
Ralph Abrams [Palizzio, New York] and Bill Sheskey [Com-
monwealth Shoe & Leather, Whitman, Mass.] can only
work at NSI part-time, but we've been able to bring NSI to
a new high in money and men participating.

"What good does it do the little fellow? Sears doesn't need
NSI. We have our own resources. The same is true for all
the big companies. We are able to do our own promoting,
publicizing and educating. It's the small guy who would
benefit proportionately much more from an expanded NSI.
For he's the man who, under present conditions, is too small
to do much for himself, and for whom there exists only NSI
with its limited program of fashion publicity."

Mr. Izen paused in his discourse. Clipped the end of his
Corona with a gold cigar cutter, and resumed. "I get carried
away some times. This business, this company are my life.

"I spend most of my time concerned with people, counsel-
ing them, helping solve spot problems when they come up. I
try to be a source of ideas. I play the role of architect in
building and shaping our business. I'm a resource developer
and a product developer.

"This is a decentralized operation. The buyer has complete responsibility in selling and marketing. It's my responsibility to measure the buyers' progress. It's not hard to
measure buyers' results. You simply follow their share of the
market. A buyer does two jobs—store selling and catalog

selling. The individual is very important in this exciting business.

"I came to Sears 26 years ago and shortly afterwards met my wife Rosetta. I entered the business world after graduating from Northwestern in 1932. Worked for the now extinct Chicago Evening Post for a couple of years. Then worked for Cutler Shoe which was sold to A. S. Beck. That was 1936–1937. I worked three years for Maling Bros. and came to Sears in 1940 as buyer of men's dress shoes. And here I am. I've loved it. If you have to work, everybody should work for Sears.

"I'll be retiring one of these days—five, eight, 10 years. I can't say exactly when.

"One of my boys, Allan, is a desert botanist in Arizona. I've a daughter, Sharon, at the University of Denver, and a son, Shelley, at New Trier Township High. He might go into business some day.

"I'm away from home one-third of the time. I'm an early riser during the week. Up at 5:30. I never eat lunch; I work right through.

"Weekends I sleep late. I don't shave. I look like a bum. I read, play bridge, watch TV. I putter around the yard. Gave up golf a few years ago. Bad back. I hate cocktail parties. I visit stores some times on Saturdays. I've been a Chicago boy all my life. Born and raised near here. It's a quiet life. It suits me fine."

CHAPTER 10

Behind the Sneaker Explosion

Louis J. Healey

THE U. S. Rubber Co. headquarters building in Rocke-
feller Center is graying and totally out of fashion in this age
of corporate super-images. Sound is subdued and the tone
in the hallways is somber. On the 15th floor, a visitor wandering through is informed by nothing so much as an air of

uncompromising formality. Institutional green. Heavy square wooden desks. The style you might call utilitarian-functional. Nothing for the eye. From one of the inner offices, the prospect is the sign atop Saks Fifth Avenue and one of St. Patrick's spires. Everything else is slab, glass, faceless. Inside, the walls are hung with reproductions—a townscape of San Francisco, the Latin Quarter in Paris, vintage cars. No wall-hung silks, flaming colors, exotic fuss. Mrs. Johnson's Committee to Keep America Beautiful has never been by. The only ostentation is its absence. Given U.S. Rubber's most recent profit and loss statement, it would be fair to assume the office has come into some neglect. Two things work against the idea. The first is a Steig cartoon on the wall, showing a dowager being fitted with a pair of dress shoes and imperiously making clear to the hapless man on the stool that she wants Keds. The second is Louis J. Healey, the man who calls the signals for Keds. [Ed. note—Until 1966, when he was appointed vice president and general manager of U. S. Rubber's plastic division.]

The cartoon establishes Healey's instinct for the world of appearances, and its relationship to Keds and the other footwear products U.S. Rubber has been putting on the market with increasing frequency lately. Healey, in his manner, bent of mind and clarity of reaction, establishes U.S. Rubber's style. It is simple, unadorned, direct. Emphasis is on the business at hand. There is no time or place for the frills. Stress the fundamentals. Impose order on them. Drill them home. The fundamentals, unencumbered with complexity; the fundamentals given priority. If there is no room for frills, it is not out of neglect. And if things tend to be understated, that is the company's—and, by osmosis, the man's—style.

"We wanted to call it Peds, but our lawyers were told by the patent office that it came too close to the sounds of some other brand names. So we batted it around for awhile and decided on the hardest-sounding letter in the alphabet, K, and called it Keds, that was in 1916."

What's in a name?

Lou Healey is neither ironic nor aphoristic by nature. Rather it's the nature of his role as chief executive of a leading factor in an industry that makes these qualities inevitable. If he answers questions about his business quickly, without stumbling, it is not because he is glib, but because he has been grounded in the fundamentals.

U. S. Rubber got him when he was a pup, as Healey describes it (a shoe pup, at that. Healey's father ran a shoe store there—and still does), the man who came East (from Santa Rosa, Calif.) while all the other young men were going West. Starting as a clerk in San Francisco in 1939, and taking time out only for 5 years in the Navy, he rose to assistant manager of branch sales for footwear and general products at headquarters in 1953; manager in 1954; general manager of the consumer products division in 1956; vice-president of the company in 1958, and divisional president in 1962.

His office 15 floors above 6th Avenue is the farthest he places himself from the marketplace. He works a 7-day week a good part of the year, takes time out only to sleep and to be with his family (wife and three daughters) in Greenwich, Conn. Clothes (black plain-toe bluchers, this day), food, pastimes are all functional. The degree he earned in college was in business administration. When he talks about his product, it becomes clear he's never stopped learning.

"This didn't happen by chance," he says. "We had a tough time of it in the late 1930s. But we got onto this idea of promotion very early. And by promotion, I mean goods at regular prices, not reduced prices. That's a misconception.

"We had a convenience item, an accessory—not a needed item—and we knew that. So we developed a partnership concept with the dealer. They sell and we promote. We went out and developed promotional devices, from the mouse circuses on up.

"The concept of promotion took a long time to permeate the organization. It had to grow over a period of years. But we kept at it. We got to the kiddies. When they grew up, we grew with them.

"If we didn't promote, we'd be in an inferior position today. We promote right across the board—children to adults—clowns, games, rides, contests, fashion shows. The idea is basic. We just adjust it to the level we're trying to reach.

"An example is this 'brilliant canvas' promotion for our Keddettes line. It's going to break in the spring. We bought an art collection, which we'll put on tour and tie in with department stores; get two or three full windows, and tie in with all the departments, working with the store's fashion coordinator.

"The pitch is on the high end. We have a product promotion team, but the ideas come in from the field as well. The idea for Kedso the Clown came from a salesman in Chicago. Let's be clear. We're selling promotion today, as much as the actual staple goods.

"How'd we know the market was there? We knew we had a good product and we kept getting the right signals. There was a gap in the market. We went along with it. We do some pilot testing. But mostly we test under cover. We're continually running tests in the Naugatuck plant with high school students—tests on new lasts, new styles, durability of various materials. We follow the age groups very closely and we study fabrics.

"We have people moving all over the world continually looking for new fabrics, new colors. Sometimes it's costly. But it's the only way you maintain yourself as fashion leader.

"We've got a terrific built-in market system, more than 300 Keds salesmen, district managers, regional managers, product managers. They're continually feeding us information.

"When we put lines to bed we're pretty well oriented in what's going on. We call everyone in. Find out what's hitting and where. It might be hitting in only two places, in Dallas and Los Angeles, say. But the minute we know that much, we know we can pick that up and duplicate it everywhere else.

"Then of course we do formal market research. We make five-year forecasts which we adjust every year. We cross check sources from our market system, and then we decide where the negatives are to be found and so on. If we've been wrong in the past five years we've been short.

"Sometimes it takes some things longer to hit than you counted on. When we first brought out blue denim, the first footwear company to do so, we thought for a few years there that we'd have to eat a lot of shoes. But the curve straightened out and turned up.

"It's a matter of blending ideas and promoting them with talent. We try to keep on top of it all the time. A year ago we had an outside market research group run a survey on our whole setup. We wanted to know what image of our brand the consumer had. We wanted to know whether we were in line on price; how many members of the family bought Keds, and the position of Keds in the minds of the public of today, compared with 1948. We wanted to learn something about the function of the blue label in brand identification.

"It was based on controlled interviews over a period of nine months, and cost us about $40,000. Essentially it confirmed a lot of what we already knew. But that was important. That gives you the confidence to keep doing it. And of course we learned from it. We learned we've been able to bring the youth along as they moved into maturity and raised families of their own.

"The brand association was very strong in the under 35-year-old age group where we had a 77 per cent positive response to Keds. Response in the 35–50-year group was more than 50 per cent. Above 50, the response fell off. We learned it's a market we haven't penetrated yet. We've been checking into this since. It's a market with obvious potential.

"We also learned that for large families, the price structure on our children's shoes was too high, the quality not high enough. It was a good investment."

The thought lingers for a second, while Healey dips into his jacket pocket for a loose cigaret and shifts gears. He is talking concepts now, low pressured, unembroidered, mixing new themes with variations on old ones.

"For us everything starts with the sale. Always has. That's why we developed the partnership concept. We don't want to haggle with our dealers. We have 35,000 of them. We simply want to show them how to see, how to move more and more goods.

"We spend a lot of money training people for this purpose. It's a constant, year-round effort. We take our people young. It hasn't worked the other way around for us. We found it extremely difficult, taking an experienced shoe man and teaching him our tricks. We would rather take him out of college, move him through the chairs, get a good look at him and his capabilities. When he's through the course, we can pretty well tell how he'll stand up to time.

"We use some psychological testing, but only as a guide. Essentially our process involves looking at him, bringing him along through the check points. We give him broad experience. We believe in cross-pollinization. District and regional managers hold regular classes on weekends.

"And we have a training school, where the emphasis is on the basic philosophy of merchandising control, quality control, promotion, working with the dealer. Fundamentals. Promotion is so fundamental with us that none of our goods are sold until we establish clearly with the dealer a schedule of promotions. Part of the order, in fact, indicates when sales are to be held.

"It's a very fast track, faster than it's ever been. That's one reason I have to travel a great deal. I've found the best fertilizer in the world is the boss's footprints. I'm very conscious of organization. That can't be stressed enough.

"We keep upgrading across the board—talent, efficiency, promotions. But we feel organization is more important than anything. Our image with the dealers is just as good as the salesman. I keep on the road half my time, seeking this goal.

"We're also continually upgrading quality. Most of the good people are upgrading. We sell a lot of shoes for $9.95. But we don't feel by that, that we're competing with the shoe industry—by that or by anything else we do. We're getting the extra pairage, that's how I look at it. I feel the leather shoe people should concentrate more on promoting what they develop.

"As it stands, they're doing business with a lot of obsolete models. If they emphasized promotion more, they could quit squawking about price. You can't sit still and expect the old style to carry you. The change of style in American life to casual living has done for us what it did for the casual people in leather shoes. Thing is, we saw it back in the postwar period, 1945–1947."

Another memory point. Healey arches forward on the couch, completely given over to the conversation. So much so that, when his secretary interrupts with a phone call from the Keds plant in Ponce, Puerto Rico, he has her put it off for a few hours. He tells her instead to bring in a couple of new styles and, as if the question had been suspended in midair, he says simply "I think you make your name by what you put into it.

"We brought out this National Football League sneaker. A built-up gym sneaker. It sells for $6.95. The canvas is done up in imitation of a pair of football shoes minus the cleats.

"There had been a 3-month sales slump at the end of the year which we couldn't turn around. We toyed with the idea for years, but we couldn't get a handle for it. We thought this could be it. The tie-up with the NFL was it.

"The response has been phenomenal. We knew it would hit in the big metropolitan areas because of the team identification. But it's in the small towns where we've been surprised. There's tremendous identification there with the teams. We provide the dealers with team decals, different ones for different regions. Plays up the identification theme.

"It's only a gym shoe. But what we've done has upgraded it, perpetuated the dealer's canvas season and excited the public. That's the formula.

"Here's another one—conductive hospital shoes." He holds up a pair of green canvas shoes, unusual only in that each has two small black plugs fused into the center of the sole, and the inner sole lining isn't padded.

"We analyzed the market in terms of need. We worked with a doctor from Waterbury, Conn. on this. We tried to find out what the objections were to the kind of footwear being sold for hospital use. They wanted something that would absorb static, something they could wash to get rid of all the blood and dirt that accumulates, and something with colors other than white.

"We developed a conductive compound. That took a lot of work. Then we had a problem getting the conductivity into the shoe. When we overcame that, we got the underwriter's approval and we were off. There is an enormous market for this shoe.

"In some other market research, we found there was a need for waterproof golf shoes. A $40 leather golf shoe is ruined by rain. We developed the Royalon golf shoe for $14.95, and it's been very successful. We're not competing with Foot Joy or any of the others in the field. They're out of our price and quality range. There's a market for this extra and we're filling the need.

"Of course, we're aware of the leather footwear industry. We follow leather shoe styles like a hawk. And some of them, we feel, have done outstanding jobs reaching their market. Hush Puppies is a prime example. Wolverine did an excellent job—promoting, distributing—they did a good job with the retailer.

"But here again, the thing was wide open. The market was out there. I think there still is a market out there which we don't wish to go after, because of the limits of our capabilities, but which the leather shoe people can get if they can excite the consuming public to the greater use of footwear.

"It's a matter of promotion and organization again. This is what has been our value to the retailer. This is our partnership concept paying off. In a changing market, we're changing with it. First we've made the canvas season year-round.

Second, we've moved into a very advanced dating program that enables the retailer to operate, in effect, on our money.

"We book August to December, shipping season runs from December to April, bills come due May 10. We'll have turned a retailer's investment on spring stock before the bill comes due. There are no markdowns, no obsolescence. This is what we promote at the shoe shows. We don't sell at the shows. The only thing we show is our promotional activities. We're there to orient the dealer to our plans for the year.

"It's imperative to us that we can do this. The flexibility of a large company is limited by the chain of command and, while we never clam up on an idea, we fairly well keep within the formal lines of the organization.

"We run forward planning meetings once a quarter. This is where we predict where we're going. We discuss product development plans. If timing is right, we review lines. We bring in the development, production and advertising people. Ideas that were kicked around on the product level are reviewed. We set up deadlines. This is necessary for production scheduling.

"But if someone has an idea at any level at any time, and we think it can hit, we try to cut into the schedule to get it out. We've become sensitive to this as we've become more susceptible to change.

"That's the difference between business now and 5 years ago. We are in this world of galloping change. Everyone has to recognize it. We no longer can sit back and say 'we have a market.'

"Before the war, 65 per cent of our business was in gym-type sneakers. They're still the foundation of our business, but they account for only 35 per cent of the volume now. The pace of the change has quickened. There's more variety. Styles live shorter lives. Fads, the status business, are good examples. Very volatile business. But it's important to follow the trend. For this you have to be flexible.

"We're experimenting in our plants with shorter runs. We've introduced the express checkout counter idea, where we can make short runs of all kinds of items, at the same time interrupting the schedule whenever necessary. If something is hot we can move right in. We don't have to wait 2 weeks anymore to schedule it.

"The pace is quickening and it's become all the more interesting. [The 1966 market for canvas footwear, including imports, is estimated at 211-million pairs, compared with an estimated total market, exclusive of over-the-shoe footwear, of 1 billion pairs.] I like the challenge. Our growth in the past few years has been sharp. Volume has gone up about 15 per cent a year on average for the past 5 years.

"We may have been lucky about competition, but then when people catch up to you in staples and you know there's only so much the market will bear, you move off into other areas. The Desma process has made it somewhat easier to come into the industry, but on the low end.

"Our concern about the Desma process isn't the competition, however, but the quality of goods it feeds into the market with which we're connected. It's this 98 cent stuff. When you get the mark of poverty on something you lose your appetite for it. That's the only deterrent to the canvas footwear market—the look of poverty.

"We've been through that before, though. You get away from it by styling, new lasts, innovations, promotions. There's also been a tendency recently to level off from our growth, but we're convinced it's temporary. We think the market will take another boom 2 or 3 years from now and we're planning accordingly. We've been through this before, too.

"It all comes down to the fundamentals. Most of all, I'd say the key to our business is promotion and organization. Everything follows and falls right in.

"Join the National Footwear Manufacturers Association? We've been invited. But because of the tariff battle in Washington, we thought it better not confuse the issue for the present.

"For the present we'll paddle our own canoe."

CHAPTER 11

The World Is His Marketplace

Thomas Bata

"YES, we're going ahead on the plant. I'll have to call you back on the details. What? No. The Indonesian situation is still in flux. I'm expecting a call from Jakarta this morning.

"Before I forget, will you check on the sales report from

the Ivory Coast, and send Frank in. I'm not to be disturbed for 3 hours, except for urgent calls. We'll be in the conference room."

Thomas Bata, looking a bit like Claude Dauphin, in dark blue, patterned tie and pocket puff matching, is standing outside his office peering out onto a floor as big as a field across which (almost as if it were an afterthought to dress up the empty spaces) are arranged small clusters of men and women, quietly occupied with their work and seated on and behind the kind of office furniture the New Architects design into the floor plan.

It is not yet 10 o'clock, but the morning temperature has already moved into the 70s outside, an unusual day, and the high-rise buildings in downtown Toronto in the distance, through the window of a corner office, look like Chicago off the Lake. The leaves in the surrounding countryside have just started to turn color. The scene inside and out is all of a piece.

"Dr. Herz," someone calls to a small, dapper man approaching, "This way." Bata finishes what he's saying in private to four men, all looking very alert, listening intently. They check their watches. Two move off quickly in different directions. The others follow Bata into the conference room, a kind of brooding isolation cell, big enough to play war games and which indeed suggests nothing else. Colored flags dot a ∟ap of the world spelling out where trouble and its possibility exist on the globe.

A movie projector peeks out from behind one wall. Alongside runs a panel of names, executives en route to one of the 55 countries in which Bata has business holdings, or on the way back to World Headquarters in Toronto, Canada.

Above, ceiling-high and running horizontally across the length of a wall are two rows of small rectangular panels divided into the time zones of the world. It says all that has to be said about the company. As the panels light up, the top blue ones representing waking hours and the bottom red ones representing working hours moving across the row a rectangle at a time, inevitable and unyielding, a visitor has the uneasy sense of movement without moving. For Tom Bata makes clear the continuity of a day's passage around the globe is a matter of course.

"Why don't you ask me a question and we'll see if the tape picks up your voice?" London is back from lunch. New York is about to take a coffee break. San Francisco is still asleep.

"Why'd we buy Weinbrenner?"

He fixes his eyes on a distant point in his mind, looks over at C. K. Herz, Bata Canada president and head of Bata North American operations, lets a smile of complete tolerance relax his strongly-drawn features and begins to talk, measuring his tone with a deeply resonant voice, deliberate almost to the point of physically fitting the words to his thoughts.

"The main factor was that we'd expanded at Belcamp to the extent we no longer had a supply of people. In this I think we weren't unique. And we had the alternative of not expanding anymore, building some more plants (elsewhere) or making some acquisition. We'd heard Textron was interested in selling Weinbrenner. It didn't fit into their program, but it was parallel to ours, so it seemed quite natural.

"They were in a much higher price range than we'd been in but which we'd been trying to get into. When we saw it, we were impressed by the product. We were impressed by the people. We were interested in a successfully operated organization. If it hadn't been there, we would not have made the deal.

"Textron had done a tremendous job of introducing good

things from a management systems point of view into Weinbrenner and we felt we could make a contribution from the technological viewpoint. We felt it would be a much faster development than if we started building new plants somewhere else.

"This was a very unusual thing for us to do. We'd more frequently buy some distributing organization. But, very very seldom have we bought a factory. In fact, the last time we did was about 1940 when the Germans were invading France and one of our plants was in the line of German advance and our French executives bought a small shoe company in southwest France to have some place to go in what became the unoccupied zone of France. Of course we lost that, too, to the Germans. I don't believe we've bought any shoe factories since, until now.

"Does that sound right?" He looks to Dr. Herz for verification. Dr. Herz, a lawyer, with a degree in political economy, and a key figure at Bata for more than 25 years, nods in agreement.

"We bought Weinbrenner for among other things, as I said, to break into the higher-priced men's field. One of the features of the American market is that various brands or various companies tend to operate in various strata of the price range. In Europe this isn't so common. There's a much wider spread.

"There are elements of specialization. In the United States one of the basic reasons for the success of the economy is its concentration on a narrow field of activity. Or it was until the entrance of the diversified corporations. But basically these diversified corporations still do specialize and I think they try to excel in that particular type of activity and I think it's a very good thing.

"But from our points of view, our leather footwear opera-

tions, has really grown as an adjunct to our rubber and canvas footwear which automatically is in the lower price ranges
and therefore automatically the leather footwear tends to be
in that range too.

"Now we don't want to go into the high-price by any
means. We want a medium-price field. And we'll make very
fine shoes for the purpose. Most of Weinbrenner's activity
is in the middle market. We've no plans to extend our reach.
We reckon there are fine opportunities to work in areas in
which we now operate. On a worldwide basis, most of our
emphasis is still on the lower price. The highest price area
we're in is Western Europe. But this is a relatively small volume.

"In the developing countries, we have to start from the
premise that the individual has got very little disposable income and that he then goes to where he can buy a good product at the lowest possible price.

"In most of these countries our shoes would not be the
lowest in price. Some local manufacturer would be the lowest priced operators in a relatively small volume. But then
there's the question of quality versus price. We try to put
into our merchandising in developing countries first class
quality.

"In the long run, those people who have very little disposable income have a much longer memory of their experience than people with large amounts of disposable income,
like in the United States. To Africans and Asians today, and
to other low-income groups, the purchase of a pair of shoes
is sort of equivalent to an American buying an automobile.
The investment comes into that sort of category and therefore if he's satisfied, the customer is going to come back.

"In developing countries, the economic purchasing power
is small. But the growth potential is tremendous in many of

the areas. The advantage which the whole shoe industry has in the developing countries in particular is that one can start small if it's a virgin market.

"So we have started, as a rule, in a very modest way— feeling our way in each country. Our initial investment could be very small and we could give it more support as it gets going.

"On a number of occasions we've gone and started in one of the developing countries with very little hope of profit— certainly from a short-range point of view, and I should say we did it partly because we felt that as an experiment in some kind of sociological activity we should do it, and I should say it worked well wherever it's been tried.

"The Sudan is one example. The Ivory Coast is another. Those were places where the government offered incentives to get a factory going and have some nucleus of industrialization which they could then show to others in the hope that others would follow. In most cases it worked out extremely well.

"The incentives? Well you see, they will give tremendous incentives such as 5-year tax exemptions which look terrific on the surface, but if you make nothing for 5 years having started in a modest way, and you start making money only when the tax holiday is over, the incentives don't amount to much in terms of profit. But more important, they are an indication of the atmosphere in the country more so than a gift of money.

"I have found that the political atmosphere is of primordial importance in economic development of any country, whether it be the Ivory Coast, Canada or anywhere else.

"The few places we've had to retreat have been where political problems occurred. We're very hardy, however. Yes, we have a plant in a suburb of Saigon, a place called Chong, and I think we operate at the moment about 50 retail stores there, all doing well. We hope we have no Viet Cong in our employ.

"There is some idealism in our approach. We feel we are making local raw materials through local labor into products locally consumed. But I should say this. For many years, I've been a Rotarian, and Rotary has a motto: He profits most, who serves best. And every time we've done something which had some kind of idealistic flavor to it, it has been a good thing.

"I'm quite sure American shoe companies are capable of organizing a business in a developing country. I don't believe it takes special wisdom. And I wouldn't want to say we know more answers than United States shoe firms. We admire our competitors too much. They are so doggone smart. Many of them have much better gross United States sales than we have.

"How long it would take them, I think, depends on the attitude of the individual. I think investors in these developing countries need a tremendous amount of enthusiasm and a little bit of adventurous spirit. I don't believe you can operate a business in a developing country effectively on a part-time basis. You must, literally, speak the language. That will be true for each country you go into. That's very hard for somebody who has been brought up with the one-language system.

"The biggest potential market is of course North America. But in terms of spending power only. Take India. With a population of somewhere around 500 million, the shoe consumption is roughly 100 million. So you've got 400 million people who do not buy shoes. Now just to put one pair of shoes or sandals even on the feet of one Indian per year is 400 million pairs. What's the total pairage of the American shoe industry? [United States footwear market is about 1 billion pairs. Ed.]

"We have 150 stores in India. It's our biggest operating unit. The people don't have money for shoes now. Yet there are tremendous industrial areas developing. A fertilizer plant goes up, creating thousands of jobs and immediately people have cash in their hands with which to buy all kinds of material goods. So when you say 'biggest potential,' you must be aware of all sorts of nuances."

Asia has been the lodestar of Bata dreams for more than a generation. Thirty-five years ago, a New York Times reporter in an interview with Thomas Bata, Pere, described how the founder viewed Asia's uncounted millions as potentially a two-pair-per-capita market.

The elder Bata was one of the most famous business innovators of his day. He bore that sobriquet, "Europe's Henry Ford" and the title seemed well merited. At the age of 18 in 1894, as a young shoe worker, he set himself up in the shoe manufacturing business. After a decade or more of treading water, and with a couple of years in the United States and Germany learning the most advanced production methods of the day, he returned to his native Czechoslovakia town of Zlin with the aim of making a great, national industry of what was then (and still is in some places today), a somewhat imprecise and helter-skelter business.

In the depths of the Great Depression, Bata employed 18,000 people and made 134,000 pairs of low-priced footwear a day in Zlin that penetrated virtually every market. American manufacturers who competed with Bata in those days still speak of the experience with some asperity.

Bata was an early exponent of flying and it was to cost him his life in a crash in 1932. That disaster, compounded by World War II and the Cold War, dealt the Bata organization a series of staggering blows from which it fully recovered only within the last few years.

Bata left a hastily drawn will which appeared to leave working control of the company to his half-brother Jan. But Bata's widow and her son, the present-day Thomas, sued to recapture control in a series of lawsuits that spanned two decades and two continents. The litigation ended in 1962, somewhat anticlimactically, in the venerable Court of Chancery in Wilmington, Del., with the filing of a paper and the payment of $1. The token marked the transfer of control of the Swiss holding company that in turn controls Bata, from Jan to Thomas, the son.

Meanwhile, the gigantic industrial complex devoted to footwear production in Zlin had long since passed, first into the hands of the Nazis, and thence to the Communists, and the center of Bata power had trekked westward to the tranquility of suburban Toronto.

Thomas Bata, the younger, speaks of today:

"We're not heavily into the American market, but we've been growing quite rapidly since 1945 from a relatively modest size and it's been a steady growth. The American market is a very difficult one to operate in. I think the difficulties are primarily involved with increasing consumption. My feeling is that France, for example, probably has a consumption of 2.5 pairs while in the United States consumption is well over 5. To increase national consumption above 2.5 requires much less effort than to increase it above 5.

"When you increase per capita consumption, you're taking business away from some other product. In the United States that's hard to do. That's a much tougher job than to fill a vacuum. There have been other limitations to our being more strongly into the American market. Adequate personnel is one. Possibly, money is another. The Weinbrenner acquisition is an indication that we intend to keep growing in the American market—not by taking the bull by the horns, but by shoving him forward."

"Our plans in the United States have nothing to do with operations elsewhere. We're totally decentralized. Each individual company in the organization works at its own operating policy based on local conditions and circumstances. For example, the British company operates on the policy of not owning any of its buildings. It leases its stores. Bata, Ltd., the holding company, tries to own all the major buildings we're in. The British company some years ago said that it would buy those locations which it could not otherwise acquire by lease. After a while we reviewed this, and decided we weren't in the real estate business and did a lot of lease-back transactions.

"We did at one time do much more of trying to consolidate matters and then we discovered that, actually, from a working point of view, this is a dangerous thing. That is, very often, it tends to false security. There's always a weak link in the chain.

"Our function here in Toronto is almost like a trade association office. For the Bata people in say, India, we're primarily management consultants. We found we can influence the operations of the Indian company in a very small way. We can help provide them with new technology.

"We can provide them with training facilities to send their people into various parts of the world, with marketing information. We can provide them with a tremendous volume of service. Service they would not have if they weren't part of an organization. But from a normal operating point of view, there is very little (in Toronto) to do. The job is done entirely in India.

"Even if it's a question of moving into a new level of the

market, the decision is made in India. We might bring them in here, talk about, make information available, hold conferences, courses. We would, in short, do a solid job on it— soft sell or hard sell depending on how convinced we were that it is a good thing for them. We would not pass the borderline of a hard sell which would contradict the management consulting relationship, however. Here is an example:

"We thought a particular line of plastic footwear would do well in India. The management of the Indian company decided against it for many years simply because they looked at it and said 'What is the foreign material content?' They found that the foreign material content was 85 per cent of the product. They disapproved.

Now the situation has changed profoundly. During the last 3 years, PVC materials have become available from local Indian sources made entirely of local material.

"Suddenly from an Indian economy point of view it is better to make footwear out of plastic than to make it out of rubber. India produces a certain amount of rubber, but still a large portion of rubber consumed in India has to be imported. So the swing immediately occurred. The decision to a large extent was in the hands of the Government. In fact it became Government policy that this type of production be reserved for small-scale operations. So what happened was that they licensed about 15 different small firms to buy this PVC equipment and we are not making this type of merchandise, although we have got distribution agreements with a group of the companies.

"Decision-making on the corporate level, at Bata, Ltd., here in Toronto, is a committee function. We have a number of committees for various types of activities. Frank Maltsby our technical consultant, for example, shortly will be holding a meeting in Europe on technical developments, which will be attended by key people from various companies. The decision as to whether a new machine would be developed rests with that committee. The same holds for personnel change.

"We're prepared to move people from anywhere in the world to anywhere in the world. Of course we sometimes strike the problem that their wives are not prepared to move anywhere in the world.

"We have an American running our Canadian company, a Frenchman running the Brazilian company, a Canadian running the Sudan company, an Englishman running one of the French companies and a Frenchman running the Belgian company. In the top echelons and in the specialty fields 99 per cent of the people working in each country are nationals of that country. But we believe in cross-fertilization. Our display room is a good example.

"The 'display room' is more like a trade fair than anything as mundane as its name implies. Stocked are styles from 55 countries, in every conceivable shape, color and material, reflecting culture as much as economics, all of it accessible to the roving eye. The cross-fertilization possibilities almost suggest themselves.

"That's a very practical approach to merchandising. We also try to use computers. They sometimes complicate our lives fantastically. Trouble is they don't design shoes. That's where the key is. We don't have any magic mix to tell us how to be sure what we order is going to sell. I think we're groping in exactly the same way toward this as everybody else.

"Basically, what we try to do is to make as nice, smart, progressive shoes as we can in every country and sell them as effectively as we can.

"I think we have the advantage of some large insights into

production technology. And we probably have some advantages in putting into a market values which are superior in many directions to others. Secondly because we're so decentralized, we do attract quite a variety of progressive young people. And finally, because of our involvement in developing countries, we enjoy a sense of adventure, a sense of pioneering to a certain extent—doing something for more than money, the great feeling of pleasure which one gets where in a wilderness, you can see a new industrial activity developing.

"You see the people who participate in it enjoy a standard of living which is incomparably higher than that of their brethren. To some extent, you even stimulate others to come with investments. More industrialization takes place. A community develops.

"Of course, at that point, strong unionization is inevitable, industrial ferment, and everything else. Civilization, you might say.

"Closer to home, in Canada and the United States we see our expansion in two directions. One is work and the other is leisure. In both areas, we're going to try to think ahead.

"We see a big potential in better types of these shoes, hunting footwear, casuals, the whole range. We're going to go increasingly into more sophisticated types of products."

The traveling lights click on. London is just closing down. At the precise moment, a call comes through from London. "Goodnight, London."

"We try not to wake people up at 3 a.m. their time. But if some problem arises, it doesn't always work out that way. But it works reasonably well."

San Francisco is having breakfast. It's 5 a.m. in Calcutta.

"I travel a lot. About three to four tours around the world a year. And then I spend probably about two to two-and-a-half months a years in Europe. But that might be part of a tour of India. I'm experimenting with a different system where I do more air miles but do not spend quite that long on tour. But it still takes a long time to get from here to here and one says to oneself, 'Allright, I've already gone so far, I might as well go here to here to here, and another four weeks is gone.'

"The traveling does help, however, to give one a picture of an overall nature, rather than a narrow one.

"There's one great advantage in this sort of thing I do. There's no routine. Never a dull moment. And its guaranteed that if there is some very serious problem, something else will come along to take my mind off it. If I have trouble sleeping, which isn't often, I find that if I concentrate my mind on one of the challenging opportunities, what some people might call problems, I find it almost a refreshing state. It puts me to sleep.

"I love the outdoors. I play tennis and I try to ski occasionally. Reading? I read Footwear News. Books? I manage to read a few, not as much as I would like. Ian Fleming, mostly. I wouldn't want to say that I have any particular literary taste. I go more for topical and professional things.

"I'm on the board of a ballet, but I'm not sure that I make any sort of contribution. I look terrible in tights. I'm on the board of a new university which I find challenging.

"I hate to say that probably I'm a very 'conservative' dresser during working hours and probably very casual during nonworking hours (boots, cowboy hats and dungarees). When I'm traveling I make a point of trying out bits and pieces, but not very frequently. I have fun trying out shoes. Today, in fact, I happen to have two shoes on of the same kind. Very often my left might be somewhat different than my right. But I do try to be a clothes adventurer while setting a reasonable appearance."

Tom Bata, and his interests—business and otherwise—around the world are the products of modern European history. Nothing much more remains to be said about it. World War II left the Bata business empire in havoc. The Cold War and the Iron Curtain reinforces the loss. When he came to Canada he was terribly young, terribly impressionable, terribly under the influence of America.

"Why did we put down in Canada?

"We came in 1939, after a long run across Europe. The clouds were gathering there. I had to think of the future.

"I had read all kinds of stories about people from the Wild North and Jack London and so on. I'd gone to school in England and the United States and my father being a great enthusiast about the United States, I was brought up in almost a United States kind of atmosphere. And since I also liked many of the British ways and I had been given to understand that Canada was sort of halfway house, I came to Canada. This is how it all really started."

Part Four

A Quartet of Elder Statesmen

CHAPTER 12

The Man Who Understands Mommies

Samuel
Slosberg

MILD-MANNERED, almost bland, he can also be incisive.

He says, "Anyone can make a good pair of shoes.

"The captive account is more likely to tell you what you want to hear.

"Anyone can make promises about delivery. We tell our men not to make rash promises, and make damn sure we can fulfill the promises we do make.

"We've made every mistake in the book."

This is Sam Slosberg talking—chairman of Green Shoe Manufacturing Co., head of the biggest company manufacturing quality children's footwear in the country. The man who understands "mommies." At 69, still going strong as the specialist's specialist in the special business of making and selling children's footwear—at a handsome profit. (Return on invested capital, 14.9 per cent in 1966.)

A short, gray-haired, gray mustachioed man, his modest appearance belies his success. He could be taken for the owner of a successful jewelry store. Carefully dressed, he comes across slowly with a disengagé quality.

"When this business was started, we decided to concentrate on high-grade children's footwear. We decided to make enough footwear in sizes, widths, styles and colors so that the retailer could count on us to deliver what he ordered. For, in order for the retailer to give good fit, he has to have the right size.

"Now it is one thing to set out on a determined course. It is quite another to stick to it, to work so diligently that the retailer can count on us to fulfill our promises. Anybody can make good shoes. Anybody can make promises about delivery.

"Fulfilling promises—that's where the real work comes in.

"In the high quality field, we have something to give the retailer and the consumer. The mother can rely on us. If you go to a store and buy a suit, looking only at the price, you have nothing to rely on except the price. The mother wants, for her child's feet, good fit. We give her that, we promise her that—and if by some chance she doesn't get it, she can come back to us and make good our promise. This is the advantage of the quality field in children's footwear.

"Oh, we've looked at other companies in the footwear business. We have the sneaker line now (added in 1964), but what we want in a firm is management. Too often when you examine a company, you find that everything revolves about one man. He may be in the best of health, but he can walk out in the street and get hit by a car—and there goes your business. (Mr. Slosberg mentioned a known brand manufacturer, whose president was stricken a few years ago.) I wouldn't want to have acquired that company, everything in that company revolved about that key man.

"We are not merely in the shoe business, but in footwear apparel, anything worn on the foot.

"We are always talking here about ways of expansion. I think there's growth right here in the children's footwear business. Oh, the birth rate may be falling at the moment, but it will pick up and our population will expand. In addition, there are further areas of growth in children's footwear apparel."

The company HAS grown. Since 1955 sales have almost doubled, and profit has more than doubled. In 1960 the company went on the New York Stock Exchange; in 1962 acquired Weber Shoe Co., and in 1964 bought R. J. Potvin Shoe Co., maker of babies' and infants' shoes under the Buntees trademark. In 1966, it acquired H. Scheft Co., a retailer, and in 1967 the Blue Star Shoe Companies.

What's the position of independents today?

"There's all kind of talk about the decline of the independents, but we think they're healthy. At one time independents constituted 35 per cent of our business, and department stores 65 per cent. Today it's 60 per cent independents, 40 per cent department stores. When I talk about independents, I include those with two, three, four, six stores.

"Today the shopping center developer wants the independent. It used to be that the developer sought only those stores with AAAA credit ratings, and this meant only chains. But this also meant, usually, that the developer did not get the stores with personalized service. If the developer wants a higher grade store with personalized service, this means he will want the independent with a good record, good brands.

"Because so much of our business is done with department stores, we learn about new shopping centers two years before the buildings go up. So we are in a position to help the independent get in on the ground floor. When we hear of a new center on the drawing boards, we tell our retailer in the area about it—and we expect our retailer to go into it. We practically demand it. We also help him if he needs help in getting in."

How do you keep in touch with what the consumer wants, since you don't have stores of your own?

"One thing mothers are concerned with is proper fit for their children's shoes. Mothers worry about this. Proper fit means having enough sizes, it means not double sizing—that is, having B and D but not C. We don't let our retailers do this.

"We had a sales meeting here a short time ago, and present at that meeting were several retailers—a buyer for a big department store and a small independent. They keep us informed of what we don't learn elsewhere. The captive account, on the other hand, is more likely to tell you what you want to hear.

"We're not in the retail business—and when I see how much the retail end of the business gets on dollar sales, I'm glad we're not in it." (Green Shoe netted $2,558,982 in 1966 on sales of $43,983,289, a 5.8 per cent sales/profit ratio.)

"We are very close to the retail business because our prosperity depends on the prosperity of our customers. Our salesmen are merchandisers, not order takers. They know everything there is to know about retailing, because it is vital to us that independents be successful.

"Our salesmen tell the retailer when to size up, and when not to size up. When a retailer does get into financial difficulties, the most frequent cause is poor inventory control. He may be good on the sales floor, but he's not keeping up with his books."

How's your new line of sneakers?

"They've been introduced, and this coming year we'll see how they go. When we introduced our Stride-Rite sneaker, we put in quality which no one else had, and offered them at a higher price. I always like to play to the other fellow's weakness, not his strength.

"Now they've raised their prices and increased the quality.

"The trouble with the shoe industry is that too many people are afraid to ask a good price. They sell themselves short. What this industry needs is more self-respect.

"Mothers are willing to pay any reasonable price to take care of their children's feet."

Will synthetics ever have a place in children's shoe uppers?

"Corfam or a similar upper synthetic may some day be perfected for children's shoes, but not now. And we've tested them all. None has tested out. I don't think synthetics have got to come. I like leather."

*As the son of the founder of your company, do you agree
with the view, expressed by Clifford Anderson, that sons have
a more difficult time working in their father's company?*

"Yes. A relative, such as a son, in a company is liable to
get a harder time. He's got to prove himself—perhaps more
than a non-relative.

"This gets into the whole problem of nepotism. The president of Green Shoe has proved himself—he also happens to
be my son-in-law. The executive vice-president of the company has done great work in leather buying, very smart
fellow—he's my brother's son. I don't think that a man who
is born into a family business should be denied the chance
to prove himself in the business. But he does thereby have
a rougher row to hoe.

"At the same time, as regards relatives in the business, top
management often has some tough decisions to make. Some
relatives sometimes don't work out as they want. They have
a certain capacity, which they reach, and want to go higher.
But they have to be denied this opportunity because they do
not have the qualifications.

"Management after all has the responsibility to stockholders, to the board of directors, to the future of the business—and these cannot be placed in jeopardy through hiring
or promoting unqualified relatives. This sometimes involves
hard decisions."

Have you given any thought to retiring?

"I attended a college reunion several years ago (Harvard
'17) and we were all asked to fill out questionnaires on what
we intend to do on retiring. Very few were in the same classification as me—with no plans to retire. In a few years our

class will have its 50th anniversary—and," he paused, "it will be interesting to see how many have actually retired."

"Of course I have other interests outside of the company. I'm president of Beth Israel Hospital, a trustee and on the board of Brandeis." Other interests? "Music. I used to play the fiddle. No, not the violin. The fiddle, we called it. And I still like to listen to good music."

CHAPTER 13

The Gentle Eagle
of Lincoln Street

Philip
Lown

JUST beyond Boston's Chinatown, a street sweeper heedlessly slops muddy rainwater on passersby. The scene is Lincoln Street, the city's waning wholesale shoe district—once a sought-after address of the shoe industry, because of its proximity to South Station, now losing many such tenants because of overcrowding.

In an old office-warehouse building, the landmark num-
bered 179, are the general offices of Penobscot Shoe Co.,
which maintains its production facilities in Maine. Up the
wheezing elevator to the fourth floor and through the wide
hallways—then through the swinging gate at the reception
desk is the unpretentious office of Philip Lown, president.

Leaning against the comfortable high back of his chair,
Mr. Lown is as unpretentious as his surroundings. A slight
Old World accent flavors his calm speech:

"No company can be successful for very long unless it has
a philosophy of business. In the manufacturing business you
have to adopt certain standards of quality and stick to them.
You have to try to improve on them without increasing the
price to the customer."

"For instance, say that the edges of the sole are not shiny.
If you can find a new die to provide a better finish, it costs
you a fraction of a cent per pair—but it improves their appearance." (It went without saying that the fraction of a
cent would not be passed on to the buyer.)

Another part of Philip Lown's philosophy—"About 30
years ago I told a chain I was selling to that I would raise
prices 10 cents a pair because of a new union contract going
into effect April 1. As it turned out, the contract didn't take
effect until May 1. So I told the buyer I would delay the increase until May 1.

"The man kept repeating, year after year, that it was not
the dollars involved—but he saw he could depend on me.

"Business is not just a matter of dollars and cents—it's a
matter of relations with people."

He paused, and added with a slight smile: "A while ago,
one of the top three manufacturers asked me if I would consider a merger." Again a short pause. "I said I'm not adverse,
not adverse, to negotiations—if we could work out the right

plan. It depends on so many conditions. Similar standards of quality, and the right relations with people are so important. You spend so many hours working with people—and you have to be able to think the same way they do.

"One time I was talking with a smaller firm—yes, looking into acquiring it—and during the course of our conversations I realized that firm did business in a different way than we do. I dropped the negotiations."

Whether it's Philip Lown's business philosophy, or other factors, there is no doubt that Penobscot Shoe Co. has made a success of the specialty shoe business. Making women's loafers and casuals since 1940, under such well known names as Old Maine Trotters and Mainstreeters, Penobscot made over $1 million in 1966 on over $18 million sales. Sales were up 15 per cent over the previous year. One of the new methods with which Penobscot is experimenting to sell more shoes is going where the college students are. Asked about this program, Mr. Lown, reluctantly, explained:

"We know high school and college students are our best customers. Of course, they can buy our shoes everywhere—but we thought we could stimulate more sales if we could bring the shoes where they are—either in stores on the campus, or those close to it.

"Usually, you'll find one or two stores more popular with students than the other stores. We sent a young college graduate to do some market research—and sent letters to the president of a sorority and a fraternity on each campus—asking them what stores they go to, if they ever heard of Old Maine Trotters and what they buy?

"In 1965 we started putting our shoes in these stores on a consignment basis. The target we're shooting for is 100, but we haven't sampled out enough stores to be able to tell how it will operate.

"The shoes remain ours. The stores actually are salesmen for us, and we pay them about 30 per cent for selling the shoes. In most cases, we did not replace other lines. We advertise in college publications and supply the stores with display units.

"The young market is good for both immediate and long-range results. If we can put our shoes on them, they will continue to buy for many years afterward. My wife is over 60 and she still wears loafers. Maybe it's because I make them."

You went public in September, 1965. Did it "hurt"?

"I spent three months working on that. I knew there would be a lot of forms to fill out, but there was an endless amount of them. And then everything has to be so exact. Do you know that not every printing firm can print up a prospectus—there are only two in Boston [which can do the job the way the SEC wants it]? You have to have just the right paper, and the right type. We had to have lawyers and accountants in here—and there are ongoing forms to fill out.

"Every item must be made public, and everybody knows what all the executives earn. So you not only become a target for contributions—but also for wage increases. Also, you're not a free agent. You have to satisfy the SEC and the underwriters."

How much did it cost you?

"About $100,000.

"Yes, that's what we paid out, exclusive of the work we had to do ourselves."

Was it worth it?

As always, the ever so slight pause, then: "Being publicly

held has some disadvantages, but I'd say it's worth it. The advantages are twofold: If anything happens to a major stockholder, it can't shake the company financially—that is, if a major stockholder should die, and the company would have to buy his stock, perhaps we could do it with a large loan, but it would hurt our financial standing. If we were a privately held company, and a major stockholder died, the estate and the IRS would argue about the value of the stock. This way, we know.

"And—if you need more money, and can justify it—you can make a secondary offering, and the value of your stock can be determined on the basis of performance."

Since basics account for 60 per cent of your sales, how has this affected your business?

"The type of shoes we make are those that repeat themselves season after season with slight modifications. One of the reasons I sold my old firm, Lown Shoes, in 1963, was because I didn't feel I could be involved in both basics and novelty shoes. We have some fashion in our shoes, too. Some change every season, some every year. One season green may be strong, but it always goes back to black and brown.

"Our approach makes for good production planning. In novelty shoes, retailers take about an 8 per cent markdown. In ours, they don't have to take more than 2 per cent."

Philip Lown is one of the few top executives in shoe manufacturing who has spent a number of years running a company outside of the footwear industry. For 11 years he had his own company producing dyes for the textile industry. (When he came to the United States from Lithuania at 15½, he worked in a shoe factory and hired a tutor for an education, becoming a chemist.) A flood of imported dyes from Germany forced him to sell his company.

How did you get into the shoe business?

With a warm smile he said: "I had a relative who was in the shoe business. I thought—if he can make a success of it— I can."

You have been selling to department stores for many years. What changes have been wrought, in your view, in their buying practices?

"Of course there are more leased departments.

"Many department stores have found they're not making money on the items that require the greatest amount of skill. Why should they lose money when they can be guaranteed an income? But leased departments are not good for us. When the department store runs its own shoe department, it's not beholden to any one manufacturer.

"But when the department is leased out, it's leased out to whom? To manufacturers. When they take over a leased department—first of all, they promote their own shoes.

"I'm glad I'm in the specialty business and it doesn't pay for the big manufacturers to go into a specialty item. They have them—but cheaper." (His inflection on the word "cheaper," a long "e," told his disdain.)

He leaned down, pulled out a desk drawer, and asked: "Would you like a cigar?" He deftly lighted one for himself, and continued:

"Department store buyers are becoming much better trained than they have been. There has been too much of this situation where merchandise managers bring buyers in from other departments—instead of engaging a shoe buyer. Some of them still think all a shoe buyer has to do is go out in the market and buy. This viewpoint is changing considerably. Now there's more of a trend to promote from within the department—or to go out and engage shoe buyers."

Does selling both branded and unbranded shoes offer any particular advantages?

"Yes. It helps us keep a better gauge on fashion trends. The large, volume buyer who handles unbranded shoes has to buy earlier. Sears and Montgomery Ward already are looking toward next spring. They have to prepare catalogs and do a lot of planning."

The conversation is interrupted. But nothing is lost as the executive returns to the subject at hand. Where many younger men would resume by asking: "Now what was I saying?", Mr. Lown almost continues where he left off in mid-sentence, as if endowed with a mental bookmark.

"—When we see the mail order houses are grading up, for example, we can feel other accounts will do the same. But the big, volume firms follow the branded lines for fashion, more or less.

"When we develop a new idea, we make up some samples and our sales manager and assistant sales manager make a trip. They go to the major accounts—and when they get back, we analyze the response. When 25 smart retailers accept it, it's not entirely a blind gamble."

Do you ever introduce a style when you feel it appeals only to a limited regional area?

"This depends if a large enough sales area is represented. Some time back, we introduced black suede loafers. The largest market for them was the Southeast—they used 80 per cent of what we made in sueded leathers for two to four years, but then it grew northward.

"The area around Dallas is very fashion-conscious. I believe there are more well-dressed women there than in other areas. With the oil wells around there, they're well-oiled. They're looking for something different. Neiman-Marcus is a strong influence. New York also is fertile for new ideas."

Do you feel cooperative advertising is an important phase of manufacturer-retailer relationships?

"Yes,"—and in a matter-of-fact, resigned, tone, "They help the retailer 75 to 80 per cent and the manufacturer 20 to 25 per cent. A customer may go into a store to buy Old Maine Trotters, but will buy other shoes, too. Whether they sell that particular item or not is immaterial to the retailers.

"Unfortunately, in spite of the Robinson-Patman Act, all kinds of deals are being made." He moves into this sensitive subject without a change in inflection, and a total lack of self-consciousness.

"Some manufacturers don't take into consideration that when they're giving an advantage to one company, they're hurting another. I'm considered tough in that respect. We have a plan and follow it very closely."

What qualities do you look for in an executive?

With a trace of a smile and a faint shrug of the shoulders: "He's got to be a magician, an alchemist, a diplomat—and if he wants to be successful, he has to know he's in business for a profit. Some salesmen often are so intent on selling shoes that they forget about profit.

"We have three layers of executives—55 and up (that's just Max Kagan and I)—45 to 55—and 30 to 40. Of 10 men on our executive committee, four are related. My son-in-law is general sales manager, my nephew is manager of Northeast

Shoe Co.—and Max Kagan has a son-in-law in the business."

How are current labor shortages affecting your plants?

"It varies with different locales. Where we are—while labor is tight, it's not too bad. We invite high school seniors to our plants. We make contact with them long before they graduate. In Old Town, we don't have much of a problem because there are very few factories there that employ a lot of people.

"High school graduates don't feel secure on account of the draft—and, at times are confused as to what to do. My own grandson is, at times, a bit confused. A good percentage of high school graduates do go into the factories if you involve them, throw out some challenges and offer opportunity for advancement.

"About 80 per cent of our foremen were advanced from within. It's necessary for us to do this, because we're in a specialized business. We have handsewn operators who make $150 to $200. The average is about $3 an hour for the more skilled operators.

"About 10 to 15 per cent of our help in the Old Town factory comes from the Penobscot Indian tribe. Indians have a natural inclination for making handsewns."

How old are you, Mr. Lown?

"Do you have to—?"
A nod of the head. *Sixty-one?*
"Seventy-five."
A sprightly 75.
"A friend of mine—a philosophy professor—said it's better to die living than to live dying. I hope I can carry out

this philosophy. You've got to be active instead of being afraid you might die and then not doing anything. I have many other interests outside the shoe industry."

A sometime golfer—no longer for a full 18 holes, and a fisherman, he spends his vacations in Naples, Me. Active in educative, philanthropic organizations, he is a trustee of Brandeis, president of the Hebrew Teachers College, a member of the World Council of Education and past-president of the American Association of Jewish Education.

"If I limited my interest and time to the shoe business, I wouldn't enjoy life very much."

It's obvious that at 75, he enjoys life, including the shoe business.

CHAPTER 14

He Bossed the Biggest Brand

Joseph S. Stern, Sr.

"We're great promoters. It isn't a question of who's first, it's how you follow through that counts . . .

"We are the largest maker and advertiser of branded shoes in the United States.

"Our Red Cross division sells more shoes than its competitors.

"The Viva Americana line is the fastest growing line of shoes in the shoe industry today.

"The most trusted name in shoes is Red Cross."

Joseph S. Stern, Sr., retired chairman of the board of U.S. Shoe Corp., can go on for a long time telling you how and why his company is best.

It's a litany that everybody at U.S. Shoe chants, firmly believes in, sells to the customers, and Joe Stern, Sr., is its chief exponent and expounder.

His is the single-minded drive that brought U.S. Shoe's sales from $2.5 million in 1932 to $169 million in 1966 and made Red Cross the top brand name.

He is 75, looks and acts at least 20 years younger. His eyes twinkle and his hands saw the air when he tells you why his company has grown so large.

Ask him what are hardest decisions he has ever made and he will tell you: "Changing personnel for the betterment of the company."

What's the secret in selling branded shoes?

"You must first create a desire for your product in consumer's minds. Then you must produce a shoe that is compatible with the meaning of the brand. You must make a shoe that even if it didn't have a brand name would be the most competitive shoe available. We have tried to give a little bit more, rather than a little bit less.

"We have always believed in pre-selling our products and creating a need for them in consumer's minds. In the late 30s we participated in an advertisement in Life magazine, in cooperation with Life, on a 'Life Goes to a Red Cross Shoe party.' After that Life had 500 applications from manufacturers who wanted to do the same thing.

"We introduced our Cobbies line on the initial crossing of the Queen Mary and had a group of girls modeling our shoes.

"We sponsored the first hour long, national hookup TV show in 1956 and it cost us $156,000.

"Today U.S. Shoe spends in excess of $1 million on consumer advertising.

How did U.S. Shoe grow?

"We started this business by taking over well known respected brands that weren't doing well. We added youth, ingenuity and new merchandising and advertising techniques (Red Cross was bought in 1932, Joyce in 1955, Selby in 1956).

"Right after the war we sensed a change in consumer demand and decided to make some changes to keep in step. We believe in research. We really believe in it. We spent a lot of money on depth interviews. We found out what women really wanted to buy, not what they said they wanted to buy. We sensed demand for fashion in shoes and introduced Socialites and Cobbies to meet the increasing demands for fashion shoes and casuals for suburban living.

(In 1953 and 1956 U.S. Shoe hired research firms to study its position in the industry. The reports suggested that it seek additional lines and retail outlets.)

"From then on we decided that we would no longer take over old failing brands. Our new direction was successful firms. We agreed that we wouldn't take over an organization unless they had the best men available. We wanted men and companies who didn't need us, who could do well without us, though needless to say any connection with U.S. Shoe would be helpful. The same policy holds true today."

(Since then the company bought Vaisey-Bristol, children's shoes; Marx & Newman, Italian shoe importers; William Hahn, Washington-Baltimore retail chain; Cutter-Karcher Shoe Co., leased department operators; Princess Shoe Co., women fashion shoes manufacturer joined the U.S. Shoe family. Texas Boot Co., makers of western family boots, was added in 1966, as was Freeman-Toor Corp. A retailer, Charles Kushins came in 1965.)

What are your personnel problems?

"About 1955 we were advised that we needed a second and third line of young management for progress and expansion. We took the advice seriously and started to build along those lines. Today our expanded young team has assumed the authority it should have.

"Though we are still neophytes when it comes to seeking young college trainees, we have been conducting group interviews at the University of Cincinnati and Xavier University for some time and we are now planning to interview other candidates at other schools.

"We started this company with youth, continued down through the years with youth, and now young executives run U.S. Shoe.

"We like and need youth, but it must be youth with energy and a goal in life. Our people are aggressive and ambitious . . . come to Cincinnati on a Saturday or Sunday and you will find our executive parking lot is always crowded.

(He sets an example by the many hours he spends in his office and even though active management is now in younger hands he's not about to stop yet.)

"The average age of our executives is 40 and we haven't a man in the company who isn't hungry for himself and the company. There is no such thing as a 40-hour week for our executives. Some come in at 7 a.m. and leave at 7 p.m. and get plenty of hell from their wives.

"If there's a man in our company who hasn't been offered other jobs, he's no good. But there is a loyalty to U.S. Shoe because every executive knows he can do more and probably do it better with us than any other place."

(After talking to him awhile you realize that he is a man who must constantly be doing something. He will ruffle his papers, make notes, stand up, occasionally stop to accept a call, and when he wants to make a point his hands move in the finest Latin style.)

Are your salesmen still paid commissions?

"Of recent date we have been gradually expanding our sales force and taking more men off salary-commission and putting them on straight salary plus incentive bonuses. The same holds true for the management team, depending on brand performance.

"We are doing this because we feel our customers need more service, and by a further division of territory we are able to give customers more service.

"We also lessen per cent cost per sales. Selling our shoes isn't difficult because our brands are pre-sold, pre-advertised and there is so much customer acceptance."

What are your selling costs?

"U.S. Shoe's selling expense is the lowest of any branded line in the industry. Red Cross is about 2 per cent and the average of all our company lines range from 2–4 per cent.

"I should also point out that all of our executives sell. They all have important accounts that they call on and service."

How do you achieve your high profit ratio?

"We always plan to net at least 5 to 6 per cent after taxes. Because all of our brands are pre-sold, we can accurately forecast, even before salesmen go out on the road, the number of shoes they will sell in a 3–4 month period. As a result we definitely know what our per pair profit will be.

"We have made economies in modern techniques of manufacturing and construction. And since our products are pre-sold this allows our leather buyer to order large quantities of leather in advance at substantial savings."

What's the future of independent retailers?

"It will be rough because big suburban developments are encroaching on their territories. They give more than he can give. The pattern of distribution is changing and while downtown stores are slightly affected, the small country store in towns of 5,000 and less is being cut into. Their biggest hope for survival is to buy well known favorably received brands.

"It is impossible for an individual to go into the retail shoe business by himself today. In the past, a family would loan money to an enterprising young man. Today financing must come from large companies.

"This is one of the reasons that we established our Market Service division. To be of service to small retailers whenever we can.

"We have certain plans in mind of furthering the concept of the shoe business and all plans will be carried out for one purpose . . . a selfish purpose . . . for the more profitable operation of merchants who give us their business."

What are some of the don'ts that U.S. Shoe has observed?

"Don't put a shoe into production unless you can produce at least 10,000 pairs, except in some very rare instances.

"Don't build a company on one man.

"Don't take over an organization unless you have the best men available to run it.

"Don't open a new factory until your present facilities reach an oversold condition.

"One final and important don't . . . don't write this article as though I'm U.S. Shoe. There have been many wonderful people like Nathan Stix, our chairman, who contributed so much to its success."

Do you like vacations and what are your hobbies?

"The best vacation for me is the shortest one. If I could go to Paris on a Thursday evening and be back at my desk on Tuesday morning, then that could be fine. I'm nuts about sports, especially baseball and golf."

Are you looking forward to retirement?

"Well as I pointed out before there is a younger generation in charge of U.S. Shoe today. The compulsory retirement age is 65 for executives who have not been with the company for 20 years. In my case it was 69, but at the option of the board and myself I could be continued on a yearly basis.

"Six years ago I went home and told my wife I wanted to retire to have fun and do other things. Next morning I returned to the office and realized that I had more fun working for U.S. Shoe than anything else I could think of.

"But I realize that retirement is coming slowly and surely, and I agree with the executive who said 'I look forward with a certain degree of horror to that Saturday night when they present me with a watch, because I already have a watch.' "

CHAPTER 15

Leather Fights Back

Max
Kirstein

PICTURE a bulldog riding a roller coaster and you get some idea of the Max Kirstein story—complete with sinking sensations in the stomach.

At the moment, Mr. Kirstein, chairman of Irving Tanning

Co., Boston, was seated at his office desk being a "bulldog."
His lower lip and jaw protruded pugnaciously.

Footwear News had just thrown him a question—the kind
that sometimes causes the subject to bristle.

The question involved how Mr. Kirstein felt selling out in
1962 to the Seagrave Corp., a New York-based firm which
makes paints, chemicals, lighting fixtures, architectural products and fire engines. After all, Mr. Kirstein started Irving in
1921, nursing and nurturing it through Depression prices
("sheepskins in the '30s were considered high at $7 per
dozen skins") into a war-postwar parlay doing more than $15
million annually when Seagrave bought it.

Sure, the sale price was $11 million, with $5 million cash
outright, $2.5 million in stock and 15 year notes and $3.5
million to come out of Irving profits.

But it is not unusual to equate one's family-owned company with a child. Despite the cash sale, perhaps there is a
sense of loss that no money unguent can properly heal.

If Mr. Kirstein bristled at the question, it was not evident.
A wide smile shattered the bulldog countenance and it
occurred to one that perhaps it was just a pose. A pose en-
gendered of necessity when Mr. Kirstein, a greenhorn boy
of 15, landed here from Poland in 1913 with 7 years of tannery experience under his small belt and a lot of determination.

Neither the outspoken determination nor the accent have
disappeared:

"I have no reason to regret our sale to Seagrave. We've
been very comfortable. We've had good sales and earnings
and I don't believe we could have made the progress we have
if we had not been purchased by Seagrave. Irving Tanning
does 20 million in side leather alone now. With Kroy and
Hawthorne Tanning (both Salem, Mass.) and Hancock-

Ellsworth Tanners (Ellsworth, Me.), which we also control (Seagrave bought them in 1965), our total volume is better than $30 million.

"The leather end of Seagrave's business now accounts for at least 60 per cent of its total volume and profits and our (Irving's) earnings have been ranging better than $2 million before taxes." [Seagrave had 1966 sales of $58,543,729 and earnings after taxes, $1,415,825.]

"Why, we are making better than 60 million feet of side leather a year. Seagrave has made it possible for us to become a top tanner in the United States. Last year, we shipped 57 million feet of leather.

"My own job has changed a lot because we have increased production," [He holds the title of chairman of Seagrave, although Arnold Saltzman, president, is chief executive officer of Seagrave.]

Mr. Kirstein, medium height and physically well-set for his 68 years, took a slow drag on his cigar, which also doubles as a point maker during conversation. His cigars are smaller than they used to be, resulting from his doctor insisting he cut down. A shorter cigar is Max's interpretation of "cutting down." A mild heart attack a few years ago has done little to alter his daily routine.

He leaned back in his hard-won executive-type chair, took another puff on his cigar, gestured with it, struck another bulldog attitude and continued:

"If it weren't for imitation leather, the average pair of men's shoes would be selling at around $25. The situation is a tough one, all definitely hitched to the control of hide exports. I don't like controls and I don't think the industry likes them, but there have been certain historical times when price controls have saved a critical situation—and this appears to be one of those times.

"Without them and possibly other freezes in the form of price controls, the prices on leather would shoot up completely out of control."

In Mr. Kirstein's view, controls on hide exports are a good thing, but this one-way freeze should be accompanied by controls on the prices of shoes as well, to hold things in check.

Elder tannery statesman Kirstein well remembers how his first leather business venture went down the drain almost before it began. ("My saved-up $350 capital I thought was enough. But what does a 17-year-old boy know?") Tom Carr, Carr Leather Co., advised him and staked him to another try—this time finishing calfskins and side leather. But he switched to buying and selling sheepskins when World War I created a demand for sheepskin-lined garment leather. Irving Tanning was established in Salem in 1921, as a result.

Better off than most during the 1929 crash, Mr. Kirstein had to "sit on his leather" for several months.

"Sheepskins were sold for 3 cents a foot finished and raw stock slumped as low as 35 cents a dozen skins. Cattlehides were 5 cents and lower. In fact, you owned them at any price you offered."

When the market floor dropped out again in 1937, with Irving losing half of its capital, Mr. Kirstein decided it was time to get into something more promising—side leather. He closed his Peabody plant, opening a split cowhide plant at Hartland, Me., taking 2 years to train people on heavy upper leather.

After a few more shifts, Irving acquired Hunt-Rankin Leather Co., Peabody calfskin tanner, in 1955, merging into Irving's Maine facilities the H-R specialty leathers that include patents, fancies and grains for women's shoes and handbags.

*Do you agree with the thesis—propounded by Du Pont—
that population growth will outpace cattle growth so that a
synthetic shoe upper will eventually be, if it isn't now, an
economic necessity?*

"Yes, I think a synthetic shoe upper will become an
economic necessity—maybe a year from now, maybe 5 years
from now.

"But I don't feel the competition from synthetics has
changed significantly in the past 5 years. It has not hurt us
as much as we were worrying about. I don't think synthetics
have taken or ever will take the place of good leather, but
if it were not for synthetics, hide prices today would be 50
per cent higher than they are."

Jabbing at the air with his cigar, Max asserts he's "not
moving over for anyone and isn't going to play dead under
pressure from powerful interests in the synthetic shoe-upper
field."

With Irving's side leathers going into shoes to retail from
the $3.99 level to calfskin shoes at about $20, all the way up
to high-style patent leathers at $37, he believes there's plenty
of room for both natural leathers and synthetics.

*What percentage of your annual profits goes into research
and development?*

"We are spending considerably more on research and
development than we used to—about 10 per cent or better of
our annual profits.

"Our Landia process is one such development. For years
women's handbags took a beating on store counters and
shelves as a result of customer and employe handling. They
were often scratched and marred to the point of being un-
salable and represented a big loss item.

"The Landia process gives the leather surface a hard finish that withstands abrasion from ordinary handling. When retailer losses dropped, it enhanced a new market for Irving leathers.

"With research and development we want to find ways to keep the natural inherent qualities of leather—which no synthetic has yet been able to match—and to these add characteristics consumers have found desirable. If people want their shoes to hold a shine, wear better, resist scuffing and abrasion—then we're going to try to give them these qualities."

"The tanning industry generally has effected a tremendous upgrading in the past few years—even the small tanners.

"We have been among those who have done so. We use better materials, more labor and just generally spend more time in the tanning process. This trend will continue. Tanners will have to continue upgrading to stay in business. One of the major problems—almost across the board—is building an organization. It's not like in my early days, when one man could run the whole organization."

At Irving, "the team" in addition to Mr. Kirstein is Saul L. Stockman, president and chief executive officer (also chief executive officer of the other Seagrave-owned leather firms), and Mr. Kirstein's son Harvey, a vice-president and the treasurer.

How has the condition of raw materials changed in the last few years?

"The materials we get have improved. Most of the leather being made today in this country is much better than 5 years ago. But it is still not as good as we would like to see it. European material is still better."

What is your reaction to the frequently made charge that tanners have failed to provide technical assistance to manufacturers when new leathers are developed, but that du Pont has gone out of its way to provide technical assistance for the use of Corfam?

"The shoe manufacturer himself is much better informed today. The tanner is training himself to understand many things which he never did before. However, I don't think it's true we have failed to provide technical assistance to manufacturers."

With Saul Stockman as chief executive officer, since the sale to Seagrave, what are your duties today as chairman?

"My duties are similar, but not to the same extent. I'm taking it easy. Mr. Stockman, who is my brother-in-law, is very capable. He was a vice-president at Irving for many years. I like to go to the tannery as often as I can. I've reached the age that anything I don't like, I don't do.

"We're building a few additions (at the plants) and I'm letting out the work. I still keep a finger in every pie. I still have a few good years left. But that is in God's hands. Someday, I'll probably be a nuisance, but I hope I wouldn't have to retire."

Part Five

The Management Mystique

CHAPTER 16

Melville's Professional Manager

Francis C. Rooney, Jr.

FRANCIS C. ROONEY, JR., was born into the shoe industry, and received probably the most thorough grounding available in the industry's fundamentals. But he stands today, ironically enough, as a break with the traditions of the past.

He represents a new breed in the industry,—professional management, which is slowly but surely taking over the reins of authority from ownership management. And at 44, he represents a new generation come to power.

Frank Rooney's assumption of the presidency in 1964 of giant Melville Shoe Corp. was no less significant than Robert McNamara's taking the reins of management of Ford Motors in 1960.

Originally, Melville Shoe shaped itself out of the same mold as Ford. The idea was a simple one: Build a better mouse trap and have the market come to you. Just as Henry Ford did for the automobile industry, the late founders of Melville, Frank Melville and J. Franklin McElwain, brought the American industrial revolution to the shoe industry.

Frank Rooney seldom shows his emotions. But when he talks about this beginning, you can practically see his mind quicken. It is a story that is very much alive to him, one against which he measures himself.

"Certainly anyone who could build a company this large had to have great ambition, driven by more than the need for a nest egg or financial security. These founders of business were like artists. They painted the picture as they went along, a stroke at a time. They had a vision. They didn't have to develop a manual of procedure. And they were so close to the people they worked with these people got to know exactly what was in their chief's mind. Now business requires a bit more organization, a more professional approach.

"I consider myself professional management. We are dedicated to the development of a long-range plan that has to be based on the satisfaction of stockholders."

Taken baldly like that, the words belie the flavor of the man. As professional as he is, he is as comfortable to be with as anyone 'down home.' But neither are the words meant to put people off. They are exactly what he means. What sets Frank Rooney apart is the fact that he is a professional and that he started out consciously to reach the pinnacle he has achieved.

Why the shoe business? "I just never knew any better."

His grandfather ran a shoe store in Jamaica Plain, Boston, in the 1800s. His father ran Quabaug Rubber Co. in North Brookfield, Mass., where he was born. After the Wharton School at the University of Pennsylvania, he went into the Navy as an ensign, served aboard the battleship North Carolina in Bull Halsey's Task Force 58, from the Marshall Islands to the surrender of Japan. The John Foote Shoe Co. in Brockton was his first job in the industry. He worked in the factory, sold shoes on the road. When he felt he had to get out of Brockton, he took himself to Chicago and Florsheim, "the best post-graduate course in the shoe industry."

There he worked under Oswald Pick. "Pick did everything. It was great training under him." He styled the line, handled house accounts, concentrated on sales.

In 1953, 10 years out of school, he came to Melville as a buyer and stylist for Thom McAn. "What they felt they needed at the time was more fashion in the shoes. There was a demand for more styling after the wartime austerity."

It took 10 years for Rooney to reach the top. He moved from buyer to merchandise manager to vice-president of Thom McAn to director of Melville to president of Thom McAn to president of Melville.

The transition at Melville from ownership management to professional management, trade observers said when it occurred, was not a particularly easy one. What was involved was the realization by Melville's top two officers, Ward

Melville and Murray Rosenberg, that the market had changed, and that the company was bogged down in terms of profits because of its slow reaction to this change.

They moved themselves out of the front office up to the board room (Melville as chairman of the board of directors, Rosenberg as chairman of the executive committee, and brought in Robert Erb who had been schooled in the business as number-two man under J. F. McElwain).

Erb represented, in a real sense, the beginning of the transition. He was professional management. But he did not have the time before his retirement to move so large and diffuse a company as Melville off dead center. The break with the past, it was decided, had to be clear cut. What it meant was disregarding the normal management succession, jumping an age group, and bringing the company around to a new style of operation, installing Rooney at the top.

When the decision was made, it went all the way. When Rooney was given the reins, he was given the authority and the responsibility. The move has manifested itself in everything that Melville has accomplished since.

Fingering an ever-present cigar, a tall, affable Irishman, sometimes seated behind a desk which is noticeably uncluttered and sometimes moving around the large office that still holds many of Ward Melville's furnishings looking toward Sixth Avenue through a maze of gray office buildings, Rooney talked about the shoe business, management philosophy, the marketplace, his 24 hour seven-day work week.

"Right up to the war, Melville continued to give this unbelievable value. Then the consumer changed. Different styles came in. Fashion became the byword. The consumer didn't know the difference between calf and kid leather.

"But he became interested in how things looked, not how long they wore. It became necessary to be more and more consumer oriented. The public wasn't interested any more in the better mouse trap. They moved away from that. Today a company has to work backwards from the customer. This gets into marketing philosophy.

"This is how I'm pitching. We are fundamentally in the business of satisfying consumers. Compared to the past, we're more consumer oriented, more marketing oriented, more people oriented. Years ago, if you did have a better product and you got it to the consumer, they'd recognize it. Today its not the same. There's more competition, more concern with appearances. It requires more market research.

"Those of us who were predominantly in retailing after the war had to contend with the problem of the changing market. It wan't just a matter of recognizing it. We had to move physical plant and open new stores in the suburbs, in the shopping center. We never had difficulty getting sales. But there was a squeeze getting profits.

"We had to move with the customer. It meant not only moving stores. It meant new orientation. In most cases we went into the new locations with family stores. This made us develop a capable organization in the women's shoe business that we didn't have before.

"We also had to decide to take only a segment of the women's business. We made our appeal to the young suburban family and developed a new personality oriented to youth. It's not to say the fight is all over. But now we're on our way in the family shoe business.

"This did require capital. We did have a $12.5 million debenture four years ago and we did lower the dividend rate, although it since has been raised. But there was no real problem. Melville has always been financially sound.

[Melville plans a five-year expansion to add 100 stores, and leased departments to the chain each year beginning in

1966. The program will involve the doubling of new store and department openings from the current rate. At present the company has 1,314 units; 848 Thom McAn stores, 288 Miles stores, 178 Mcldisco departments. Funds for the expansion will be generated from operations. Most of the openings will be in suburban shopping centers.

The company in all of 1966 earned $11,191,530, a record or $3.88 a share, on sales of $234,313,064, both records.

Although Melville does practically no business abroad, it is looking in that direction and last year opened a buying office in Madrid that will serve as an observation post in Europe.]

"I am a very human and limited individual. I'm a great believer in delegating responsibility. My most important job is getting the right man for the job. After that, it's just a matter of following up, like writing letters to store managers, keeping in touch.

"The shoe business basically isn't difficult. Our organizational chart isn't complicated. We should know more about the consumer than we do, and in order to do it, I think we have to keep lines uncluttered between top management and personnel. That's one reason we're consolidating our Thom McAn facilities in Worcester, Mass.

"The important thing is to have everybody on the ball team. An open-door policy rather than an ivory tower. I get around. I don't stay behind this desk unless I have to. Franny Gleason, Spencer Oettinger and I talk out our problems and opportunities all along the line. (Mr. Gleason is head of the manufacturing end of the business and Mr. Oettinger runs Miles and Meldisco.) There are day-to-day discussions with executives throughout the organization. It becomes, after a while, a simple case of attitude, a case of defining where it is we're going, how we're going to get there."

Despite his easy manner, Rooney is highly introspective. It would be out of character for him to open up to an outsider. Although he never stops thinking about Melville's operations, he keeps it to himself. It is even with him on the train to and from Larchmont where he lives with his wife Frances (her father is Ray Heffernan, president of H. H. Brown Shoe Co.) and their eight children (six months to 14 years) in a three story, 20-room Georgian house. But he makes one exception to this professional discipline, an exception that paradoxically enough is in keeping with this discipline. Once a month, Rooney meets with Peter Drucker, the renowned management consultant.

"I bounce things off him. He's very helpful to me. Whereas I'm basically allergic to consultants, he comes up to things very well and asks questions to help me in my thinking process."

Drucker's thesis is that executives should devote more time to the future of their business, but they don't because they can't clean up today's business. All this, he claims, results from "the absence of any foundation of knowledge and system for tackling the economic tasks in business." If an executive is going to tackle the future he must get rid of "the challenges of today in less time and with greater impact and permanence."

"It's made me think a lot about where the profit lies in the shoe business. As Drucker says, there are no profit centers within the business, there are only cost centers. The profit is in the market. There are many places where we can develop efficiencies in the business. But there's only one place to make money.

"You can be a great manufacturer of shoes, and still have nothing to hang your hat on. Then price becomes your god. The fellow who's never been undersold may very well go out of business if that's all there is to it.

"Drucker has also made me think about what's important. If you talk about the problems you have, concentrate on that, you can convince yourself that you're the busiest man in the world, that you're working very hard, getting things done. But results are obtained by exploiting opportunities not by solving problems.

"I should be in a warehouse or a factory or a store all the time. But not sitting behind this desk keeping it clean. Corporate executives are guilty of this. My big job is building continuity, getting the proper people and their replacements. My other job is to ask them stimulating questions. My value isn't in building more sales volume, but in building more growth."

What does he do to relax? "This is probably my biggest challenge. I'm an unbalanced individual at this moment, trying to spend the necessary time with my family. Between the job and the family I can't have too many outside hobbies. I play golf and we have a sailboat. But I'm going to sell that. The kids don't want to sail with me." It is all said with the easy smile that wrinkles the skin around the eyes. The habits of professionalism inure against an offspring's rebuff. "We're too timid in this industry. We're timid about people. We often talk about not attracting good young men to the industry. But I think we have better men than we admit.

"I'm given a lot of responsibility to young people and it's amazing how someone with intelligence and burning desire to succeed will come up to the mark. A lot of people feel if a fellow is in his early 30s or late 20s he isn't seasoned. That is far from the case. We are living in such a quick-changing world that the only constant in business is change. Who is as capable of moving quickly in different directions as a young man?

"I don't claim to be a De Gaulle. But I think in any business there are many ways to stimulate people. This is the great opportunity in a selling organization. We are always looking for this, asking ourselves questions: How big is the market? What is the potential? What's our share? What can we expect it to be? How boxed in are we? What are the opportunities?

"It's all basic. We're not trying to send missiles to the moon.

"With Thom McAn, Miles and Meldisco, we have a three-pronged approach to the market. There is so much to do, thinking of it in those terms. The three divisions are fused now. It will be a very intimate and free-flowing relationship. We plan to consolidate our strong points.

"I think the day of the old European management is gone, where everything came out of the boss's office. And I would hope that people in the industry will start spending less time watching one another. There's still some of it. There are still people chasing one another around and around, defending price.

"It's unbelievable what we as an industry have done to maintain the $5.99 price point, taking things out of the shoe, making a mockery of the whole business.

"I think this will change in the future.

"I admire Federated and Sears for this. They seem to have watched the consumer; they experiment. We're going to be testing things. I think this is one thing lacking in our industry."

One of the few items on Rooney's desk, along with the

Wall Street Journal, Forbes and Fortune, is a motto: "Nothing will ever be attempted if all possible objections must first be overcome."

"We're attempting to build a business nobody can take away from us. And we know how we're going to do it because we are students of opportunity, dedicated to doing it. It isn't dedication to a memorial to anyone or anything.

"We as professionals know the only excuse for our existence at Melville is to increase the value of the stock of the company. That is done by improvement of profits, increased sales and more people around doing what they know how to do."

CHAPTER 17

The Dynamics of Change

Herbert H. Schiff

HERBERT H. SCHIFF sat back in his comfortable chair and slowly, smoothly explained: "Everyone at Shoe Corp. has or soon will write his own job description and standard of performance.

"Everyone within 3 years must name a man who could be his successor.

"The traditional policy of staff and line authorities is being superseded by a policy where communication and exchange of ideas can thrive.

"Responsibility is accountability and authority."

"Policy should be made at the lowest possible level."

"Any firm that doesn't recognize its own weakness doesn't deserve to exist."

If this sounds like a seminar on management, it's meant to be. It is Herb Schiff's way of explaining what his role is as president of Shoe Corp. of America and particularly the methods he has chosen to modernize the complex shoe retailing-manufacturing-discount department store and appliance concern.

When the mantle of leadership was placed formally on Herb Schiff's shoulders on April 25, 1965, he faced a problem familiar to many footwear industry companies. The company was started by his father—who put his stamp on the company; now the second generation was taking over and wanted to make its mark. Change is necessary, but every change will in some way contradict the methods of the previous generation. How to change the company?

Herb Schiff's problem is similar to, but bigger than, that confronted by other firms. The company is big: $258 million. The father is big. Small in stature, Robert Schiff is something of a legend, who built the company from one store to a multi-million empire. The son of this father, obviously wants to make his mark.

"The changes we have made in Shoe Corp. and are going to make are evolutionary, not revolutionary. We are modernizing our company, not reorganizing it.

"We believe in education, and communication. We held 3-day seminars before and after the shoe show for our senior, middle and junior management. These seminars also help us to size up our management—we respect people for the way they think and the way they react.

"These seminars, I believe, have greatly benefited management. They provide a confirmation of the known and an ability to look at a problem from a distance.

"Yes, I attended these courses for our management too. Why? Well, it's the old story—monkey see, monkey do."

What do you believe is your specific role in the company?

"My job description is written and approved unanimously by the 16-member board of directors. I believe it's my role to understand the scrimmage and to help the people understand the problem. It's my job to inspect and expect. To encourage communication and education. It's my job to learn why people are thinking what they are thinking. The greatest quality of a leader is not what he does but what he gets done through people."

Shoe Corp. has always had a reputation of giving great authority to its store managers. Is this policy still in effect?

"The store manager still has a great deal of authority. Some people are afraid that Shoe Corp. is losing its tradition of giving authority to key men. In the past, when Shoe Corp. set up a new operation it gave a man full power to run it as he saw fit.

"We are changing this to some extent, we are taking away staff functions that can be done better, more efficiently elsewhere. It is people who make profit. We try to provide people with the right tools.

"We are keeping the same basic concept on store managers. After all, the manager is the one you allow to care for your baby."

Commenting on his role in the company's daily decisions:

"If what happens daily has to go through my office, this business is sunk; because then everything depends on whether my wife likes me that morning."

Waving his unlit pipe, he continued, "education is necessary, and so is communication. Too often in the traditionally structured company of staff and line there is not enough real communication. What we at Shoe Corp. are trying to do is to provide channels of communication."

He roughed out a sketch of the traditional pyramidal company structure—and noted the usual chain of command. "What we are trying to do is to make it possible, make it easy, for this man to talk to this man"—drawing lines between boxes. "At Shoe Corp. we are working for an enlarging of channels of communication."

"What we want to do is to set up an organization like this." He drew a square to represent the president's office, and two horizontal lines on either side to represent, industrial relations (a new post the company will shortly set up) and, the legal department. He then drew five squares, to denote the five areas which would report directly to the president—which would communicate with each other.

The five areas: Finance, international, corporate development, manufacturing, all retailing. The company appointed one man, M. Robert Shaffer, to head up its shoe manufacturing, which includes 13 plants in this country and Canada making over 10 million pairs annually.

Retailing at present is subdivided, with S. Joseph Blatt, Sr., head of West Coast operations; George Hollander and Saul Kommessar, head of the Schiff shoe stores (east of the Rockies); Ed Solomon and Paul Resig, head of Gallenkamps; plus 21 of the budget-type department stores and 20 appliance stores.

Under the new corporate structure outlined, "Shoe Corp. could grow to several times its present size," he declared.

Herb Schiff—when he talks about corporate structure and management theory—rattles the phrases off almost glibly. When he talks about his father, and the business of succeeding with the business and his father, he speaks slowly, in a deeper timbre:

"I have to build—on what my father built, and to do what he would wish he could do. I want to do, what my father would have done, were he of my generation. I want to fulfill his dreams.

"It is not easy to be a son (in this position) but a privilege."

Sitting for this interview, Herb Schiff (he's known as Herb, not Herbert nor Mr. Schiff) presents a complete picture of the corporate shoe executive. Immaculate dark blue suit, white shirt, dark blue tie, he airily dangles his pipe in his left hand while he talks. On his right hand pinky finger he wears a large ring. He is elegantly shod in smooth black slipons with medallion toe.

The picture looks complete, but missing is the red vest which Herb Schiff has made his trademark. When he's presiding at trade functions as he has done at industry panels and press conferences (he has been president of Volume Foot wear Retailers Association), he stands out as "The Man in the Red Vest." A bright, bright red, it contrasts sharply with the dress of the other corporate leaders on the dais and with the rest of his own attire.

What are your criteria in acquiring new companies?

"The ability to produce a profit. Those companies which peculiarly help our business. Have we gotten any propositions lately? There's no company that doesn't get a lot of propositions."

Were you happy with all your acquisitions?

"Everything that has happened to us we are happy with."

At what consumer income level do your shoe stores aim?

"I'm sure that if you asked our retail shoe men that question, they would be glad to answer."
"We go where there is a market. Our strength is in finding markets."

What do you want out of EDP?

"We're a tremendous bug on EDP.
"I'm shortly going to take a week-long course on EDP. Why? Because I feel I have to make decisions about EDP, and before I can make these decisions intelligently I have to know—what it is, what it does, what it can do for Shoe Corp.
"What we want out of EDP is first, sales; and second, a breaking down of sales so that you can make decisions on distribution and sales."

Have you ever thought of moving your headquarters from Columbus closer to other centers of national business?

"We've thought about it. We have no plans to move, though. There are a lot of cost factors to be considered in moving. We're closer to reality (the stores) in Columbus, being closer to a division [the eastern shoe stores division] helps . . . I don't get into the various phases of our operation enough. Moving headquarters to New York wouldn't help us."

What is the state of downtown?

"There is a renaissance occurring in downtown, but nothing reoccurs the same as before. This renaissance is happening, or is about to happen, in certain cities, in certain ways. The majority of the stores that we have closed were Main Street stores.

"Getting the right location is more important than ever before. As for shopping centers, there's overstoring, over-shopping-centering, over-developing.

"Our strength is in finding markets. After all, business is built not on today but on what today produces for tomorrow."

What percentage of time do you devote to trade association matters and how do you feel about this?

"I spend about 15 to 18 per cent of my time in association or charitable work. You have a responsibility to the shoe community, to the community in which you live and to the country."

The opinion has been expressed that efforts to train store salespeople to provide better customer service is a hopeless and therefore useless proposition. Do you agree?

"Nothing could be farther from our position. At Shoe Corp. we try to give the salesperson a sense of dignity, a competitive paycheck, a sense of participation. Human beings must be treated as human beings.

"We are working on ways to improve the condition of the salesperson.

"When I go to look at a new plant, I ask to look at two things, the parking lot—where I can tell something about the workers by the cars they drive. I also ask to see the power plant, because the power plant is always at the other end of the factory and that way I can walk through the whole plant."

What are you doing to get a steady flow of new people coming into Shoe Corp.?

"We do many things. We participate in DECA. (Distributive Education Clubs of America).

Has your participation in DECA helped you?

"Bread cast upon the waters always comes back. The Bible is never wrong." Then he added, "Yes, we have a number of young people in our company organization who we got directly through DECA."

At 50 and a grandfather, Herb Schiff looks and sounds like a man five to 10 years younger, and not like a man with two married daughters. A third daughter attends college.

What is the state of the shoe industry?

"We are living through exciting times. Shoe stocks are still not glamor stocks. The industry is still not making comfortable profits.

"At Shoe Corp. we want to grow."

CHAPTER 18

Portrait of the Celebrity as Shoeman

Harry
Karl

HARRY KARL had his eye on shoe biz even when on vacation. Dressed in slippers, shorts and patterned silk sports shirt he relaxed poolside at the Kahala Hilton in Honolulu and spoke about his life-long preoccupation with the shoe business.

"I don't think about it really, but I'm always looking at shoes and shoe stores. It's habit. I've been interested in the possibility of a store in Hawaii and looked over the shopping centers here. I look at shoe stores and shoe departments, the discount houses also.

"There are so many divisions within the business. Not just the selling but the display, housekeeping, administration and finance. The product can be the best but it won't sell without the rest. And to keep out in front you have to keep up on all parts of the business.

"When we go out to play golf I look through the pro shop at the golf shoes. They have a lot of Corfam here. And there is a great movement in the business towards non-leather, but I like a shoe to be of leather."

The "we" includes Mrs. Karl—Debbie Reynolds. The shoe chain executive, whose name frequently appears in the columns, looks like a Southern California bank president. With hair and mustache an even silver, he maintains a serious, business-like expression, with occasionally a faint gleam in his eyes and a sliver of a smile. He speaks slowly, in a low tone:

"The 400 Karl's stores are distributed around the different states but we have split up the distribution areas with New York, Chicago, Detroit and the West Coast having their own warehousing and able to supply their areas directly." [Operated under the Karl's and Reeves names, plus leased departments, the chain does an annual volume of more than $42 million.]

"Of course, the major American shoe manufacturing is on the East Coast so it has to funnel out from there but we sell on the West Coast at the same price as the East Coast. In the shoe business the customer has a resistance to middle pricing. It is amazing. Traditionally the price point is $2.99,

$3.99, $4.99 et cetera. To try and take an item priced $3.99 on the East Coast and make it $4.25 on the West Coast to compensate for extra freight cost would just lose the sale.

"You could go up to $4.99 but that wouldn't be honest with the customer so we keep ours the same price all across the country. It is the same thing with children's shoes . . . the smaller sizes take less material but to try and price with each size jump would bring you up against that customer resistance to middle pricing. The fact that this peculiar price resistance is important was proved when one of our competitors tried to buck it and price in the middle. The result was immediately evident in their sales.

"You'd think in a business with such a volume that a few pennies per pair of shoes wouldn't make a difference over-all —but it hurt. And we aren't as big as they are so we don't have any intention of bucking the industry's set price patterns.

"Oh, we'll change our prices. We've been constantly grading up . . . but slowly. What used to be considered top price for our shoes isn't any longer. But for the last ten years we've been going up a little at a time with fashion emphasis according to customer's awareness. And according to the area in which a shop is located. We have a number of border town stores in Texas, Arizona and New Mexico which would have very different needs for fashion emphasis than stores in say, California.

"Our remodeling program is being carried out in 180 of our stores now and we'll keep going.

"There has been a great increase in volume through the 100 different discount houses where we sell, and there is less problem in this type of operation with salespeople, display and, to some extent, management. So there is also a saving to the customer. But for the big peak events . . . first school shoes, Easter and a wedding . . . that sort of thing, the families like to come into a store and be waited on and have selection. And so there is still a place for the family shoe store and that is the area where I concentrate my greatest attention.

"To me, the customer of the greatest importance is the tiniest one who comes into our store. If that parent thinks enough of us to come in with that child and trust us to fit it then I want everyone of my people to give the best service so that not only will the parents come back for their own shoes, the brothers and sisters, but the infant will grow up and keep wanting our shoes.

"A good customer is precious. Every effort should be made to keep them your customers.

"We have special training schools to instruct in fit and customer service and no one but me answers a complaint. I try and see that every customer with a complaint is satisfied.

"The retail field is the most competitive and you have to keep your customers coming back . . . nothing replaces the customer you have lost. To keep our customers we try and hire good people to serve them. And this is the most difficult of all problems.

"You can have the best product in the world, but if it isn't presented right it won't get sold.

"We work closely with fashion houses and keep with the trends. But in the shoe business you can leap too quickly so the styles for our stores are more conservative than they would be for the custom-made outfit. It is difficult to have manufacturers shifting colors. Your year-round white shoe market here in Hawaii is unknown almost everywhere else. But we show color range and keep with the fashion demand.

"Well, so they like the thong slipper here . . . I hate to

have them in my stores. They are difficult to display and don't return enough on the investment."

Conversation with Harry Karl at poolside was interrupted several times with calls to the phone or side conversations with friends but he always returned to the vital interests of the shoe business.

"The one continuing need of the business is good people. And we are constantly searching for them. I get a kick out of interviewing the young graduates who come job seeking. I could tell them how exciting the retail field is and the many sides it has. But they start off by asking me what the wages are and what the hours are. When they get through spending a lot of money on a college education they think that entitles them to a desk and their names on a door.

"They shop around at banks, insurance companies, advertising. Anything. And then at the end of the list is retailing as a last resort. They don't realize there is opportunity for fast advancement in retailing and you could work towards a position within the first year which would pay more than a whole career with a bank.

"No, I don't think the situation is any worse on the West Coast than the East. A good worker can come from anywhere and although most of our top people have grown up in the company we are constantly looking for others. [Karl's and Reeves stores are in 14 western states, with heaviest concentration in California. Leased departments are throughout the United States, except the South.]

"When we lose a good worker it is felt throughout the organization. I lost 12 stores in Watts. While rebuilding, the employes of these stores had to be relocated elsewhere. Yes, they were Negroes. Anyone who is qualified can work for me. But when these people had to go to other locations, some of them for reasons of their own drifted out of the community or got other jobs.

"A good manager is a rare and priceless thing.

"I am convinced of this by the evidence when a manager goes on vacation. The housekeeping falls apart, the customer service, stock replenishment and window display are all distressing signs that no one is in charge. It is so disturbing to me that I've even asked some of our old workers who are entitled to three weeks' vacation if they could possibly split it up a week at a time. It is simply incredible the difference their presence makes. I keep a check on all my stores. I want to know what is going on and I can spot it instantly when someone is letting something slip. And in the extremely competitive retail world today you simply cannot let things slip.

"Manufacturing? We have plants in Spain and Italy and are very satisfied with the product. Not only is the price competitive even with freight and duty, but the workmanship is superior. We aren't connected with any manufacturers here or in the Orient, although we import from manufacturers in the Pacific.

"We're getting some beautiful shoes from Spain. The factories we do business with there today are as modern as those in the United States. We're contracted for all of their output, but we allow them to do about 10 per cent of their business with other firms. Only a fraction of our volume is done in shoes from Spain, but it will increase as years go on. Cost is the main advantage.

"The disadvantage is in having to buy the shoes so early. We buy only staple merchandise from these factories. There are some staple shoes you can run for a long period of time."

In 1965 Karl's ended an experiment as a rack jobber of tennis shoes to supermarkets.

"Personnel in the markets themselves were not accustomed to shoes per se. This was an item that didn't strike their fancy. They actually ruined it (the experiment). We couldn't control it on the personnel level. They wouldn't go back to the stock rooms when they ran short of merchandise.

"We're strictly retailers," he said when asked whether the chain has any further plans for distributing or rack jobbing. Asked to comment on an experiment under way with two Fed-Mart discount department stores in San Diego, where Karl's supplies merchandise but not personnel, he asserted:

"We lease these departments. The only difference between them and other leased departments is that they supply the personnel. We handle merchandising and pricing. We may do this in other stores on the basis of this experiment. The results have been excellent.

"The personnel—when they get paid by the man who owns the store—have greater interest in taking care of the department. If the man running the department is busy, he can call someone from the men's department if it isn't busy. This cuts overhead considerably.

"When the personnel are employed by us, they're considered not part of the store group. Pilferage is much less when the employes are part of the store itself. Some employes will steal from a department owned by a large company because they don't feel they're stealing from their own company. If they work on a profit-sharing or volume basis, they know success of a leased department has no effect on their own income.

"Consumer theft is becoming increasingly worse. When you have a 3,000 or 4,000-square-foot department in a 100,-000-square-foot store, people tend to pick up merchandise and walk around with it. It's not always a matter of dishonesty."

Answers to personal questions come slowly. The matter of succession was obviously something Harry Karl had been thinking about a great deal.

"Yes, I've thought about going public, but I like owning my own business. I enjoy the feeling of it being my own business and of not having to account to stockholders.

"But one of the problems of an individually owned and managed business is that of succession. As you get older it seems you give more thought to what happens to the business later than you do to day-by-day problems. I think a great deal about what will happen to the company. I do have children but it is too early to tell if there will be any continuing interest in the shoe business. My father started Karl's in 1905 and I'd like to see it go on under that name.

"Merger, I have thought of, and I'd be more interested in that than going public. It would work out best in joining a company not already in the shoe business: A diversified company which would be interested in keeping Karl's as a separate company. We have terrific management now and it would carry on smoothly. Under such an arrangement, no matter what my heirs decide to do with their finances, Karl's would continue to exist.

"Our sights are set for someday offering the company to the public or to some triple-A company. I have the largest independent shoe retailing firm in the country. Next to me, the largest independent owned firm constitutes a difference in volume of about $30 million.

"I'm not a young man any more—but I'm not exactly old. I would never want to retire particularly. I'll be 53 in March, 1967 and have a lot of years ahead of me.

"But for now I just couldn't imagine being retired . . . or

even operating another business on a smaller scale. People suggest I might let up and relax but I simply can't conceive of living any other way. I realize the problems of management might be similar in a smaller business or some other type of business, but this is my business and I enjoy running it.

"The retail business is immensely exciting and there are many ingredients. But the most important ingredients are three . . . service, honesty and giving the customers the commodity they are paying for. I can't give them an $8.99 shoe for $6.99 but I'll give them the best $6.99 shoe there is."

CHAPTER 19

Captain of the Mighty Brown Team

Monte Shomaker

MONTE SHOMAKER, a serious, solid man, speaks softly and carries the presidency of the nation's premier footwear company.

The 61-year-old executive is the fourth president of the long-lived and puissant Brown Shoe Co.—a deep-blue chip operation which has elevated the making and selling of shoes into a major industrial enterprise with sales volume of $300.5 million in 1966. The company is still in a rising growth curve, operating on a foundation of executive strength in depth and a history of astute management of capital.

Although visibly proud of his company and its position in the industry, Mr. Shomaker can still be a master of understatement when discussing Brown's performance. "You always feel that you can do better somewhere along the line. In the company it might be in sales or profits. Personally, it might be the golf score. But the idea is to make improvements and not get mired in second guessing. It's always best not to second guess your fellow executives, and it's probably useless to second guess yourself.

"Just because a company grows large, that does not mean that it must necessarily grow complacent or less interested in the individual. In fact the contrary can be true if the effort is made."

But size has inherent advantages. In a business "there is nothing like volume," agrees Mr. Shomaker.

(And Brown has steadily pumped up the firm's volume to rank near the midpoint (number 258 in 1965) of Fortune Magazine's 500 largest industrial companies in the country. Two other footwear industry firms rank higher (Genesco, 99 and Interco, 173). The company produces about 32 million pairs a year with an approximate breakdown in pairage, of 60 per cent in women's; 25 per cent in children's and 15 per cent in men's.

Twenty years ago Brown was a fair-sized shoe company with sales of about $75 million. In the next 10 years the firm reeled off a dozen acquisitions (high points: Wohl, 1951;

Regal and several small manufacturers in 1953). Brown needed production facilities for capacity expansion during this time and six small shoe firms were acquired. G. R. Kinney Co. was purchased in 1956 (and divested under an antitrust court order in 1963). Brown's volume had jumped to $219,000,000 in 1956 and the internal growth coupled with the acquisitions had almost tripled the company's volume in a 10 year period.)

In recent years, Brown's growth pattern has been almost entirely internal. The company held talks with Rawlings Manufacturing Co., the sporting goods firm, but no purchase was consummated. The only outside acquisition during this period was the purchase of Samuels Shoe Co., upper end women's specialty firm, in the spring of 1965.

Brown's high volume mark was registered in 1962 when sales hit $323 million—then the next year saw the Kinney decision enacted and a volume rebuilding process was successfully generated.

But Monte Shomaker credits the intangible for much of Brown's tangible successes:

"The men who manage the operations of this company have a great attitude toward their work," he says. "It's a little more than concentration—I guess you would have to call it spirit."

The husky executive with the deep voice almost sounds like the coach of a ball club as he describes the process of putting together a group of men with complementing executive talents.

"It's obvious that people—good people—are the backbone of any successful effort. This company started many years ago, possibly back in 1945, with a concentrated effort to build a strong team of executives.

"The building of strong management is not happenstance,

you see. It doesn't come about by accident. It's like a puzzle
where all the pieces have to fit together or you end up with
a blank space. One of my jobs is to see that the company
gets the best men and that they use their talents to the best
advantage. No blank spaces."

Mr. Shomaker and Clark Gamble, chairman of the board
and preceding president both joined the company in 1919.
Mr. Gamble came up through the sales division and Mr. Shomaker rose through the manufacturing ranks.

"I'm the old man around here," he noted cheerfully.
"Most of our other people are all youngsters—that is, long
on experience, but short on age." (Three of the members of
Brown's executive committee are in their 40s: W. L. H.
"Hadley" Griffin, and W. F. Barber, Jr., executive vice-
presidents; and Ben Peck, president of the Wohl division.)

Mr. Shomaker relaxed at the head of a massive, mahogany-
toned meeting table and discussed the decision-making processes at Brown Shoe Co.

"We arrive at major decisions in this company by thorough discussion in our executive committee meetings. No
move is made on the basis of one man's decision, but it is
always a process of give and take. We do a lot of home work
on the problem and force the situation through a great deal
of discussion. Actually, decisions come quickly enough with
this method and mistakes may come less often.

"Everything in the industry is moving faster today . . .
manufacturing, styling, planning . . . quick decisions are
necessary. But correct decisions are more necessary."

This affable corporate leader more often reveals warmth
in his voice and actions than by a broad smile.

He likes people, ideas that work, and a wide range of athletic activities. In his youth, Mr. Shomaker had been a promising minor league infielder before an injury turned his

talents to a business which perfectly fits his name. In historical corporate sense, he is now batting in the cleanup position.

The graying executive settles back to field deftly a series of questions about Brown and the footwear industry. He thinks first before firing back the answers.

Granted that Brown's corporate decisions are a team effort, the company has made a number of advantageous financial and expansion moves through the years. Is there a particular management knack or set of principles you follow?

"I think we must realize that no matter what type of company is being managed—$2 million or $250 million—that the basics of management are similar. You must set up certain guidelines or directions for the firm. But this does not mean that there is only one way to reach an objective. Several companies can get to the same goal through different methods even within the same industry. The important point is that all the management group understands what the direction is to be. And that there is coordination between all the efforts. No cross purposes."

Why has not Brown been attracted by the prospects of diversification?

"We've had the opportunity to acquire a number of companies, but we have not found anything outside the shoe industry that would precisely fit into our operations. We used a good deal of the money made available by the Kinney divestiture to repurchase our own stock. Why? Because the potential and earnings of the stock made it the most attractive investment for us—an investment which reduced the capital structure and helped in our program of rebuilding the earnings of the company. Actually, we are neither for nor against diversification as such—but any part of our expansion must fit into the over-all pattern of our company. We have no desire to spread our management too thin."

Regarding the Kinney situation: is there any part of that outcome which was good for the company—in retrospect, that is?

(Brown acquired Kinney in 1956. An antitrust suit by the Justice Department was fought to the Supreme Court, which ruled against Brown in June, 1962. In 1963 Kinney was sold to F. W. Woolworth Co. for $39 million in cash and $6 million in notes.)

"Definitely yes. Although we disagreed wholeheartedly with the decision on the case it forced our company to make some hard core decisions. We wanted to restore our sales and earnings and although it was obvious that we could not restore $100 million in sales very quickly—we did launch a program.

"We followed three points: The most important aspect of our volume reconstruction was the giving of each segment of the company a responsibility for restoring a certain amount of the corporate volume and earnings. Happily, nearly every segment of our operation came through very well.

"At the same time, we also launched a company-wide emphasis on increased efficiencies. We tightened up all the operations. The response to this program was exceptional.

"The third point in the program was the repurchase of our stock."

What are some of your thoughts regarding the relationship of the retailer and the manufacturer?

"We try to make a constant and conscious effort to give the retailer what he needs to make his business prosper—

and these are not idle words. We've made improvements, I feel, in our communication facilities and in many of our retail programs. It takes more knowledge to be a successful retailer now than it did a decade ago—that's one reason for our Independent Retailer (IRD) program. We, as manufacturers, can help the small independent in securing a lease, setting up the business—and then guiding him with the experience that he may need. But it's still a people business— and not a counting of heads. The retailer gets an advantage and the manufacturer takes no risk—if the people are right.

"The company works very hard on trend anticipation. It is much more difficult now than 10 years ago, for instance, to see where a trend is going. We have a certain coordination in our management level with Joseph Bradley, our vice-president for development. We try to keep close to the customer and to develop young men with talent who can present the styles which the consumer will want."

(Brown's anticipation of upcoming trends is based on a combination of market research, inter-company communications with retailers and "retail thinking" sales executives. The concepts are designed to keep the manufacturer as close to the consumer as possible. The sales divisions make an effort by way of periodic letters and memos to keep their retail accounts aware of trends. Return information from the retailers is digested and analyzed in the sales divisions.)

Your career has ascended through the manufacturing ranks. What is the next important trend in achieving higher manufacturing productivity?

"I don't believe it will be any one thing. It's a series of operations, materials and technology that is pointing the way. I feel that this revolution will ultimately help in changing the comparatively low earnings in the footwear industry.

"Research and development is important. Brown started a program in R&D in the late 1940's and we are now placing more emphasis in this area.

"But there is no way to really predict what will happen in the next few years. I could not say what share of the market that synthetic uppers will have because that would depend greatly on what happens to the leather market."

Will the import situation ever be solved satisfactorily?

"Oh, there are hopeful signs on occasion. The wage scale in Europe is on the move, but the import flow is still a problem. We are trying to control it, but I do not know if it will truly be solved any time soon."

What effect does the international situation, the Viet Nam war and those implications, have on the running of a major shoe company?

"Of course, the international situation has great implications. We can foresee a tightening in the labor market and other complications. Possibly more taxes will be generated, but these things affect everyone. You can't prophesy in these situations—you just have to manage under the circumstances as they arise."

Does Brown hope to eventually encompass all price lines from the highest to the lowest?

"It is difficult to say what may happen in the future as the direction of any firm depends on market trends and price movements. However, we feel that there is tremendous growth potential still available in the mid-price ranges—the points of our current strength. No saturation point has been reached. We try to pinpoint our merchandising to fill a vacuum. But there is a great deal of room for expansion in what we are currently doing.

"This same theory applies as the reason why we have not entered other market categories like the sneaker business and the import business."

It is understood that Brown's concept of a successful new brand is one that must generate at least $10 million annual volume in the first five years. How does an operation make this type of projection? What's Brown's batting average?

"We do sometimes project on a five-year program. The key to the situation is to gather the finest market information possible on a very broad base. We use samplings, retail projections and generally try to get as close to the thinking of the consumer as possible. Fortunately, we've never had a major brand effort that misfired. Naturally, we have had to restyle lines or reorganize a concept to get the most acceptable product." (Brown has 35 brand names.)

The last price increase caused no problems in the market place. Do you expect the upcoming increases to have the same smooth sledding?

"There was no way to avoid the last price increase and the same situation is now facing the makers. But it is too early to get specific on the extent of the increase or what effect it might have. Shoes have always been a bargain item —and I think the public realizes this fact. There have seldom been pricing problems and we have movement in certain categories throughout the years."

Brown is one of the leaders in the industry in the use of art in your buildings. You have the gigantic mural in the main building and now the new leather sculpture in the new Wohl Building.

"Yes, I think the art work we have is distinctive. I'm certainly not a connoisseur—not at all—but I do think that the industrial art work we have commissioned gives a heightened interest to our buildings."

What does the future hold for Brown Shoe Co.?

"A company, no matter what the size, is set up by management to run at a certain pace or rate. I visualize Brown moving into more of a position as a leader, an innovator, as well as a maker of fine shoes.

"We are making some strides now. The leisure market opens new doors and we have entered through the men's stylings to try to find a way of increasing the men's footwear share of the apparel dollar.

"On some segments we may try to move faster—on others we may find that we are paced just right. Once more, it is a decision process which is determined by a great many people weighing a number of factors."

Part Six

Fashion: Lifeblood of an Industry

CHAPTER 20

The Enjoyment
of Fashion

Z. Albert Joseph

Z. ALBERT JOSEPH'S office is in the basement of one of his stores. It is bare-walled and unimpressive. Joseph sits behind his paper-cluttered plain old office desk looking as if he is in the wrong place. His clothes are finely tailored and he gestures with a cigaret in a long white holder. His shirt is distinctive with thin, blue horizontal stripes. He speaks articulately with a resonant voice.

Upstairs there is a finely furnished living-room type salon —the shoe stock nowhere to be seen. A parallel occurs to the interviewer—Joseph is the salon, his office is the stock-room.

Al Joseph is a man who makes money retailing high fashion footwear. There are few like him in that respect. It is a risky business for most—not for Joseph. For him fashion innovation doesn't start when the manufacturer's salesman calls with a trunk full of guesswork. Al Joseph is way ahead because he studies and has faith in the consumer.

"Let the consumer be the factor of choice. You can learn from her on a day-to-day basis. Then you can express yourself in the market without danger.

"We've underestimated the consumer for years. She sets fashion by relating to the merchandise presented to her. She doesn't know the phraseology or the language of our trade, but you can tell by her reaction what appeals to her.

"I say her, but it's the same with men. It's a crime the men's wear people don't do the same. A few, though, are starting."

His method of taking some of the mystery out of successful fashion innovation has made him one of the few who do a really big job in fashion at high prices at retail.

Joseph Salon Shoes, Inc., of which he is president, has eight salons in the Chicago area, and one in Beverly Hills, California. Present volume exceeds $5 million.

The Joseph business, founded by his brother Irving N. in 1927 when Al was going to Lewis College, started with innovation and has continued since on the same track. The original operation, Joseph claims, was the first shoe salon (living room atmosphere, no exposed stock) to be opened in the United States.

Joseph's is no longer alone in the shoe salon business, but that's all right with him.

"People in the fashion quality business are not concerned with competition, because they welcome it. If they (competition) do a good job, they contribute."

Al Joseph today believes that shoes shouldn't be such a separate business. He talks in terms of an all-over look— "things that belong together." He laments that women buy an article and then must go from store to store to coordinate.

"In Europe they do a better job because the shops are more intimate. In the Orient I observed shops where one could buy a coordinated wardrobe in a small shop at one sitting. American women who travel recognize this and that is why travelers do so much shopping abroad.

"Here we try to do things on a large scale. The stores are large. The stores make it difficult. Salespeople can't take a customer from department to department. Buyers go to the same country but in different directions only hoping that their merchandise will relate. The consumer must go to different floors to complete the ensemble. There's never been more than a fairly good job done in this country by any retailer in this area."

On this premise, Al Joseph has taken action. Some 2 years ago he opened the firm's first all-over boutique. The results? "Beyond our highest expectations."

It has ever been responsible for accelerating the shoe business in Joseph's other stores, he says. It will, of course, be expanded. "We will do it right. We have on the drawing boards plans for new shops slowly but surely. Eventually we will have boutiques in all our stores."

The ultimate in retailing, as far as Mr. Joseph is concerned, is for a person to be able to obtain for herself an all-over look in one place—merchandise that is planned, bought and shown together.

"We may find a leather color that no weaver is making. Taking the plunge is expensive because you must order a minimum of 500 yards to have something new made for you. But, we find it ends up in a profit.

"Once, while traveling in the Orient, I became fascinated with pearls. I bought $10,000 worth. It took us eight hours just to match the colors. But, this was interesting for our customers. The romance of the pearl. They were a good prop to enhance the appearance of our shoes."

As one of the leading fashion shoe operators in the country, what are his views on the troubles that have beset the women's fashion business in recent years?

"A lot of people feel the way to merchandise fashion is to concentrate on one thing. Actually, variety in fashion is great. Not any one thing is right in fashion." He suggested that anyone who takes the trouble to get the consumers' views will discover this quickly.

Another view is that the fashion shoe trade gets more quickly in step with the growing affluent society. "Grading up is the byword."

Joseph has other theories about fashion.

"Fashion is an individual expression. Fashion is a way of life. Many people have many ways of life . . . their own pursuits, surroundings, friends, recreations, entertainment. Their clothes should denote the kind of lives they lead.

"There should be variation in fashion so that people are not limited, nor restricted by dictum or trend, to wearing something that doesn't suit their way of life.

"The consumer is fashion and I believe that fashion for her is her selection for her way of life . . . that allows for freedom of choice, freedom of expression and philosophy of life.

"Once people determine what their way of life is, they should select the kind of clothes that are proper, in their estimation (not theoretical but practical) to their way of life.

"People are becoming more mature, more secure. They are not a lot of sheep, to wear clothes that are contrary to their way of life.

". . . I have made a close study of the customers who come into our shops and I see a young spirit, especially among young matrons, away from the beaten path. Until now she's had a tough time trying to find clothes that suit her and her way of life. Certainly, the teen department isn't the answer for her. I have an idea that these young thinking people are going to find themselves finally, in a position where they can find apparel and shoes to express their moods and mode of living.

"We need more people in the industry who are more closely oriented, associated and related to the consumer . . . than the operator who merely wants to ring the cash register."

The lowest price shoes at Joseph's are Barefoot Originals. The increase and growth in his business has been in the quality, higher price ranges.

Joseph feels that casual shoes must be a separate category.

What does he consider an adequate turn for his type of operation? "We try awfully hard for a 3 times turn. We haven't hit it yet."

Mr. Joseph is a man of many parts in his various operations. Some have proved him a genius, others something less. A plan for a string of franchises, with several actually in operation in the West, is now being discarded.

"We're planning to give up franchises. It's hard to control

these people. They start injecting their personal necessities. So the image is not Joseph."

The Joseph image is a key ingredient. It takes time and effort to obtain. It becomes a problem in expansion, since new personnel can't acquire it overnight. Mr. Joseph has strong feelings about this.

"The success of a business depends on people. It is one of our greatest problems. So few young people are coming up who want to make retailing a career. They are turning their backs on the need for liking what you're doing in order to make money quickly. And another thing, if you can't get your people to live together and all share the credit, then you are in trouble."

Another part of Mr. Joseph. He has a close relationship and connection with the Wolff Shoe Manufacturing complex in St. Louis, but prefers not to discuss the details.

"We started working with Wolff over 20 years ago. We needed a manufacturer who could carry out designing for our personal store needs. We found them more than anxious to comply with our demands. They thought it would be good for them, too . . . give them a closer insight to retail reaction. The retail point of view is very important to the factory.

The arrangement with Wolff began in a partnership of Al and Irving Joseph called Design Associate. It had its origin in a World War II shortage of nylon stockings. The brothers devised a shoe which permitted comfort to the foot without stockings, and called it "Barefoot Originals." The rest is history.

Mr. Joseph, it is known, has a royalty arrangement with Wolff on Barefoot Originals and the Van Eli collection produced by the manufacturer.

In the trade they say these royalties are very large and a "substantial" part of his income. When pressed, Mr. Joseph could only say that "substantial" is an indefinite and relative term and that he wouldn't put it that way. " 'Lucrative' would be a better word."

Mr. Joseph, a former president of the National Shoe Retailers Association, is a busy man. He always manages to make the rounds of his stores once a week. He likes to take a "bird's eye view" of all ends of the business.

"It's hard for store managers to be objective," he says, explaining the weekly visits. "Guiding an organization continuously depends on staying with the times."

He advises his associates to be constantly on the lookout for movement ahead . . . the consumer is fashion . . . quality is part and parcel of good fashion. Words like design, fashion, silhouette are the terms that come up as he discusses his love for the business.

They have already carried through to the next generation. Al Joseph's son, Dick, who went out on his own at age 21, has since risen to the presidency of I. Miller, a division of Genesco, and is by any measure successful in his own right in the quality, fashion footwear picture.

Mr. Joseph goes home each night to a house on the shore of Lake Michigan in suburban Wilmette. His wife, Diane, everyone says, is one of the most beautiful women in Chicago. Since Mrs. Joseph's profession until their marriage was ballet—performing and teaching—the larger part of their recreation time is spent in that art form. Inside their new home a practice bar is mounted on a mirrored wall.

Another enjoyment of the Josephs are their children, Jill, 8, and John Allen, 6.

CHAPTER 21

The View from the Top of the Market

David Dulberg

"**Y**OU must have a sound merchandising concept to operate with, you just can't run a way-out fashion business. Often you must do things that may mean a deliberate mark-down, but you must take a stand because it may be the start of a fashion trend."

This is how David Dulberg thinks a better quality women's shoe retail business should be run.

If further identification is needed he is buyer and merchandiser of better women's shoes and casual footwear for Saks Fifth Avenue and its 21 branch stores and during the course of a year he buys more high-priced shoes than any man in the country and possibly in the world.

A man nearly 61 who only feels his age "when a dull period comes along," he is easy to talk to, possesses and uses a fabulous store of fashion know-how, and soon conveys to a visitor his love of fine shoes and his constant search and consuming passion for quality.

Seldom seen without a shoe in hand, a constant observer on his selling floor, a frequent visitor to his suppliers' factories, a yearly visitor to Europe's fashion centers, Dave has been with Saks since 1929, except for a 10-year stint with Kaufman's as shoe buyer. In 1954 he took over his present duties.

His pride in Saks becomes apparent as he walks through the stock area (which peaks at 70,000 pairs), and pulls out box after box to show the depth and color assortment in any one style. When he reaches the selling floor, perhaps the largest in the world, he becomes keyed up like a racing horse approaching the starting gate.

The selling area is a sight in itself, where salesmen are sometimes surrounded with shoe boxes, showing a "live" customer the latest. He carefully treads his way along the aisle, greeting an old customer, offering advice to a salesman, picking up a sales slip: "This is excellent—over $500 in one sitting."

Then pausing a moment, drawing on his unlit pipe, he points out the variety of customers being fitted and remarks:

"Fashion to me is not just a word. It means serving a

variety of tastes and not just a small group of customers. We can't say that every shoe must have a round toe, because we serve too many customers with different needs. And if we did say that the round toe was it, then we would become static, because then you have too much sameness and no variety.

"We try to be style leaders rather than fashion followers, because our success has been built on this concept. We achieve this by being in advance of a trend.

"One of the fallacies is to overlook the basic concepts and go way out on extremes. You must stick to the middle and yet do all those things that are important to perpetuate this business of ours.

"Just look around this floor. Today's direction is the young look. Everyone thinks young. A woman in her late 40's or 50's is not an old woman. She retains her figure, wears a size 8 or 10 dress, and God forbid she graduates to a size 12, this immediately calls for a strict diet.

"Unfortunately all women can't wear the young look. They may be very conscious of their knees and can't wear shorter dresses. True they are younger, both physically and mentally, but nothing can be done about their feet, they deteriorate as one gets older. Today's customer wants young shoes but she also wants shoes that fit. We try to give her sophistication rather than the go-go look. There aren't too many 60-year-old women who would look good walking down the street in a pair of Courrèges boots.

"High fashion must be edited, because you must shoe customers according to their figures and way of dress. We offer a subtle approach to the young look. Look at these shoes, there isn't an old one here. These are average ticket items of $40, certainly not for teenagers. I don't know anything about the $12 to $16 shoe business. Ours is for the young matron to the woman in her 50's, and sometimes over, and I classify all of them as young.

"There is one thing I must point out. Eddie Cohen, who is now retired, opened this department in 1924 and is solely responsible for its success. He was followed by Manny Gerton and then Bill Warner, great shoemen.

"Manny had great vision and daring and fortunately for him he had manufacturers at his fingertips who could do what he wanted fast. In those days there were about 225 shoe makers in New York, mostly small firms making hand-turned shoes. There were vast areas to choose from because they were not copyists, were individualistic in style, and each contributed something to the total.

Has Saks' relationship with Roger Vivier been successful?

"Yes, very much so. We have attracted a new and younger trade since we have carried Vivier's designs and name. We are happy with him and he is happy with us. When he comes to New York he goes into the Lauer factory, feels at home, and he is such an artist that he can translate his ideas from a sketch to a pullover to the finished product. He visits us about once a year and I see him on my trips to Europe. And, incidentally, the same holds true for our relations with Ferragamo."

Some people say that your operation has developed an older woman flavor?

"I want to deny this emphatically. People who say that are not aware of what we are doing. We do more than most stores today. Perhaps they say it because we do such a big business on simply designed silhouettes, on lasts not accepted in the fashion world today, but accepted by our customers. I've heard these comments before and they always irritate me. Our coverage is so broad that people lose sight of the fact that we are a total shoe operation.

"We are not a small Madison Avenue shop. We cater to a tremendous variety of customers. Here's a shoe (holding a Vivier style) that serves conservative and fashionable customers by changes in materials, ornaments and straps.

"That's why I admire Dave Evins and Seymour Troy so much. They realize that women want good shoes in good taste. A lot of shoes today are designed by people trying to direct the world to a new fashion. They are thinking ahead, which is wonderful, but we must ring the cash register. If you want to be able to do these new things, you must be able to ring the cash register today."

Why are markdowns necessary on some fashion items?

"They are the icing on the cake, the window stoppers that draw attention. We know that not many customers may buy them, but they create conversation and you need conversation and excitement in this business. Think of it this way: You buy a group of shoes for display purposes to get people to stop, look and talk about what you are doing.

"They are also directed at the woman who wants something completely different, a limited edition, a conversation piece. Holding up a Vivier mule in velvet with a 9-inch bejeweled tongue, he says "Now take this for example. It sold for $65, we stocked it as a way-out item with the feeling it was going to be a markdown. It surprised us by selling well. You can't play this business completely safe . . . you lose your fashion image and stand for nothing."

Your suppliers complain that you place too much stress on quality. Why is this?

"We most likely return fewer shoes to manufacturers because we are very demanding at the onset of our buying. Saks' stress has always been on quality and service. We have very discriminating customers and we can't and wouldn't try to fool them.

"Now we are entering a new generation of buyers who don't know what quality is. Mothers used to take daughters shopping with them and point out the fine points of a shoe or dress. Today daughters are not getting this advice. They shop alone, have very little concept of what quality is. Too often today women judge shoes by price alone instead of the shoes themselves.

"We stress the fit of shoes, but we are not in the orthopedic business. Our salesmen have been taught the importance of fitting shoes to the foot, rather than the foot to the shoe.

"The American woman has been to a great extent spoiled because we convinced her to buy by size. Now it is often difficult to fit her because she wants a certain size and with the variety of lasts and styles available today, she may often need a different width or size than the one she is accustomed to."

Are you still receiving quality merchandise from your suppliers?

"We are closer to manufacturing than any other buying organization that I know of. Personally I have always loved the manufacturing side of this business. One of the scary aspects of the situation is that of the really top manufacturers left in New York, I can only count five who turn out a quality product. And I doubt if the quality of these firms will continue into the next five years, because they have a problem. It's no secret that their trained shoemakers, their specialists, are retiring, dying and not being replaced.

"Saks buys from every top fashion house. But manufacturers today try to do everything, have a little of this and a little of that, try to copy what the other fellow has and have not become important in any one area. We try to buy deep on the items we like, and as a result get the best possible merchandise."

What is Saks' connection with M. Lauer & Sons?

"Saks has no financial interest in them, if that's what you mean, but they have been making fine shoes for us for almost 40 years. Everything done at Lauer clears through the store, and we try to keep the factory running at an even pace. The problem of getting the factory over seasonal dips is always present. We don't always accomplish what we want in this area, but we try to give them advance shoes for the coming season to level off production.

"This is a sore spot with me because we have so many small factories that depend on us. I hate to say it, but some of them rely on us for survival.

"In the Lauer factory I insist that shoes be made of the best materials and well, no detours, no simplification or elimination of steps that reflect in the final product. After all you can't build quality with a slide rule.

"Incidentally on this matter of quality, the European quality shoe industry is in the same condition as ours, and we brought it on ourselves. We go to Europe and look for cheap prices. Fine shoes are becoming a lost art in Italy, for example."

What do you consider a good turn for better shoe departments?

"They are doing a good job with two turns and a 2½ time turn is Utopian. In the past we could expect and got 2½ and

3 time turns, but this was because buying habits were different."

Do past performance and record books guide your buys?

"Looking at past performance was fine when 80 per cent of your business was in basics. But past records can only be used as a guide and not as a buy book. This is just as true for other stores as it is for us. The trend has changed and you don't see the Gypsy oxford customer any more."

How do you buy for branch stores?

"We used to bring the managers to New York, give them budgets and allow them to buy what they thought best. In the last six months we have eliminated this because it was impossible to get complete unity of thought on styles. Now we try to make each store completely representative in fashion. We give them fashion and directional items and then basics."

Are good salesmen hard to find?

"Getting young people into this business isn't easy. We used to use the seventh floor as a training ground, but it presented problems for them and now we sometimes have to go outside for help. This will become an increasingly serious problem in the coming years for Saks and other shoe departments, because people are retiring and it's becoming increasingly difficult to obtain replacements. We have some people with us for 35 to 40 years.

"We have people doing well over $15,000 a year on the sales floor, including several women. Those who earn this pay have established a following, which means continuous and often large sales. Our New York staff is on a commission basis and that is unique. They are paid on an 11 per cent basis. That is, they received a draw that continues for the first six months of a year, then if their selling costs are under 11 per cent their pay rises. The lower their selling cost, the more money they make."

Why do you spend so much time on the selling floor?

"In our discussion of fashion there was something that I forgot to mention and it is so important. We have always been at the mercy of the person on the fitting stool. If they take an aversion to a new style, it will never be shown to the customer. Give me a well-trained, well-oriented staff and I will show you a staff that sells fashion.

"That's why I'm always on the selling floor. I spend more time on the floor than any other buyer I know, and I insist that my assistants do the same. I learn nothing sitting at my desk. It's important that I be available to the staff, talk to old customers, greet new ones, give advice, help a salesman with a difficult sale, and most important observe what's going on, what our customers want and are wearing."

How do you spend your spare time?

"I love gardening and woodworking and love to putter. It relaxes me and I make a point of not taking my work home. I built a sewing room for my wife Lee with lots of closet space. We have been married 37 years and it doesn't seem like a long time with one gal. My grass is like a putting green, and last summer we fed a good part of the neighborhood from our vegetable garden.

"I also like to golf when I get a chance, but since time is limited you can call me a number one duffer. On vacation we usually stay home or take a quick trip to the country, but I don't like to sit around doing nothing."

CHAPTER 22

Making Fashion Pay

*David
Evins*

"T OO many designers try for press clippings rather than orders. My basic premise is that we want to make X amount of shoes that are basic and will be reordered."

In a segment of the industry that has been moaning for years about declining volume, and doing little about it,

Dave Evins stands out as a man of refreshing candor. He is straightforward about his work and the problems of the quality-fashion shoe business. He doesn't pull his punches when he talks about fashion—how it can be profitable and why so many designers and retailers are not sharing in these profits.

As the chief designer and president of Evins, Inc. (over $4.5 million volume in 1965) he balances high fashion with soundly-based business practices. He and his company make money in the notoriously low-profit, high-risk fashion field.

Perhaps his most outstanding talent is that he is adaptable. His manner and vocabulary change to meet each situation. He is as much at ease discussing fashion with a wealthy matron as in discussing the latest factory equipment with a salesman or a lasting problem with an operator.

"I try not to get carried away by fads and fancies. They're excellent for window dressing, but in the final analysis our customers must make money on our line, and this doesn't happen if we load them down with fads that don't sell."

"Something I learned a long time ago is that I can only exist if the shoes I design are profitable and accepted by the customer. Otherwise all my sketches might wind up in the Costume Institute of the Metropolitan Museum of Art. I try not to be egotistical. Sometimes I have an inspiration. I sketch it. Perhaps make a shoe. But I have a morgue of sketches and shoes. I get them out of my system, without having to sell them to our customers."

"I must admit that I have something extra going for me that most other designers don't have . . . my brother Lee. He's my safety valve. We overrule each other. If I were working for myself, I most likely would be a perfect designer, forgetting that I have a factory, labor costs, etc.

"Lee looks after the factory and sales, and sometimes both

of us take a design out and get reactions from retailers and consumers. If there is strong acceptance then we may add the item to our line. Lee is a pretty good salesman, one of the best."

Dave Evins is very conscious of good clothing, whether worn by women or men. His own suits are by Kilgour & French, Dover Street, London; his shirts come from Hong Kong, and his shoes are made by Dave Evins, and together they create a conservative image. At 55, he could pass for a banker rather than a shoe designer.

Smoothing his graying hair he pauses a moment to consider a question on what makes him successful. "Perhaps my secret is that I design shoes that go with clothing. I have been fortunate in finding retailers who understand what quality and fashion mean, and who understand clothing. Stores like Neiman-Marcus, I. Magnin and I. Miller, to name a few, understand these important factors, and makes selling and promotion a lot easier.

What is the value of fashion coordination?

"I have always worked closely with dress designers. A lot of them are my friends and I understand their language and what they are doing.

"For years when designers introduced their creations, the models wore any shoes available. I persuaded Norell, Galanos, Trigere, Blass and Zuckerman that if they wanted to show their clothes to the best advantage, then their models should be well shod. This all helped create the picture of the shoe being an integral part of the wardrobe.

"I'll talk to Galanos over the phone. He explains his ideas and I will turn out perhaps a half-dozen sketches in keeping with the ideas he outlined.

"Some time ago I came out with a refinement on the tradi-

tional children's strap look, which I called the Sally Sandal.
I showed it to retailers and they weren't exactly excited about
it. Bill Blass used it with his collection and it became one of
the most important shoes in our line.

What's wrong with the women's better shoe business?

Leaning back on his couch, carefully inserting a cigaret
into the gold holder that is his trade mark, taking a sip of
coffee, he ponders the question for a few seconds and then
lets himself go.

"There just aren't enough retailers who aren't frightened
by quality shoes and have the know-how to sell them. Today
there are only 10 centers in the United States where there
are markets for quality shoes. If there was more retail interest
and knowledge on the subject the market could grow tre-
mendously because the potential is there waiting to be
developed.

"Today quality shoe growth is not with independent retailers, it is with specialty stores. The independent gets
frightened too early in the season, and prefers to play it safe,
which means he prefers to sell two pairs of a lower priced
line rather than one pair of our shoes.

"Shoes aren't an isolated item in a wardrobe, they belong
with clothes. That's why good shoes do so well in a specialty
store. Clothes go with shoes and the women who come into
this type of store know shoes and clothes.

"The stores that believe in quality and do their marketing
on a quality level are doing a better job than ever before. The
trouble is that there aren't any retailers joining this group.

"A store like I. Magnin continues to grow because it believes in, and promotes, quality. I happen to know, because
we are one of I. Magnin's top resources. It isn't the customer

who is afraid of price, it's the buyer. Among other things, he fears markdowns, but they aren't necessary if shoes are bought intelligently as a line.

"Price means nothing to customers if you have something they want, and to the store if it has had some experience with our type of merchandise. That's what I like about the retailers who think big and who, for example, buy alligators selling at $150 a pair. The price may shock them at first, but they realize that bags sell for $300, so they jump in and find that sales are fine.

"In today's business you can't be a designer and do it in an ivory tower. You have to be where the action is. You have to visit your stores, know the market and the customers. You just can't design and make shoes, you must offer something extra.

"We can't afford the luxury of an in-stock program, so we have to work closer with our retailers. Our rapport with our customers is much closer than that of the general volume lines. Maybe their salesmen see buyers four times a year; we often talk to our buyers four times a week."

"I have no great love for these trips, they're very wearying, but they also stimulate you because you get to know where and who your customer is.

"When I go out on the road I explain the fashion story to the customer, while the salesman does the fitting. The customer is educated, and I hope that some of the discussion rubs off on the salesman. It will help him increase his sales with other customers.

"I've made these trips since the first day I went into business. What may seem brilliant and does well in New York may not go at all in California. On these trips I catch upcoming trends, so that I am always there with the latest."

Mr. Evins started his business about 18 years ago, shortly after getting out of service. Before World War II he sketched shoes for the pattern business, where his designs were given away to bring in pattern business.

"I decided that there was a demand for fashion-quality shoes, and that I would make the finest possible shoes available in this country.

"The late George Miller of I. Miller was interested in my work and selling my shoes. When Genesco bought I. Miller, Maxey Jarman was just as interested in my work and encouraged me in many ways.

"It's interesting that Mr. Jarman, who runs a multi-million-dollar business, has always had such an interest in quality shoes and their promotion and the shoe business in general.

"He was always most receptive to anything that I came up with that was interesting and new. He always has had a feeling for creative people who do things, and has been willing to go along with them.

"At the beginning Genesco made it possible for me not to worry about finances and this permitted me to style and turn out the type of shoes I wanted."

Does Genesco have a financial interest in Evins, Inc., today?

"No, it has no financial interest in either Evins, Inc., or Delvin, Inc. (which he took over several years ago from Genesco). People can only give you support to a certain degree and then you have to walk alone.

At times Dave Evins has been a controversial figure in the better shoe industry. Several years ago some of his contemporaries were critical of his role in Du Pont's introduction and promotion of Pattina.

What are your views on such promotions?

"I won't sneer at man-made materials. Anything man-made is important. When I find new materials that will lend themselves to new types of construction and do a better job than the materials on hand, then I will use them. I try to find a new application and use it where it is most suitable.

As the recipient of the Coty award and honors from Neiman-Marcus, Kaufman's and the Philippine Government, to mention a few, he says that, "Two years ago, I turned down the Mercury Award [of the National Shoe Retailers Association] and I told them that I thought it had lost its true significance and was not worthy of true talent."

How do you create a line that's fashionable and profitable?

"The first thing you must realize is that the quality shoe business is a labor of love and you must make up your mind that you won't be as big as Genesco or International Shoe, though it can be profitable.

"When I create a line I don't think in terms of price. I build a line of about 300 shoes and after my trips and talks with retailers and customers, I edit down to 50 shoes. But I should also point out that I try to keep in mind that a high price tag doesn't mean a quality shoe.

"I eliminate the gimmicks and gadgets. I design them for my own amusement and to add excitement to the line. The shoes are shown as a collection, with retailers first selecting basics and then going on to novelties.

"I stay away from extremes because extremes always have a short life. I'll sell extremes, but I'll do it sparingly to test consumer reaction. But they won't interfere with the general line.

"The retailer's bread and butter is in basics. They can't

exist on just spot shoes. That's why I sell them a line and not individual promotional items. And when I edit and sell a line I also keep in mind the retailer and ultimate consumer, and where they are located.

"For a manufacturer to be successful in the quality shoe market you must have distribution, must be a consistent performer with a fashion story and a look and character that is yours alone."

How important are the fitting qualities of a shoe?

Fitting is an integral part of a successful shoe design. No matter how pretty it is, if it doesn't fit it doesn't sell.

"We don't sell the go-go trade. We cater to fashionable women, who are over 30, who are fit conscious, and when they get into the 40s and 50s they are even more aware of it.

"We can talk fashion all we want. The unvarnished truth is that a shoe must fit the customer. It's something that can't be promoted, it's not visual, but reorders are primarily based on fitting and not on style.

Why are soft shoes easier to fit?

"I've been hearing about them for the last 10 years. I experimented with them, but since I don't know our customers' individual weights, it can vary so greatly, you can't make a fitting shoe out of soft construction. Customers bring them back.

Why do you accept outside design and consultant assignments?

"It's a form of education, because it gives me a view of the industry outside my realm. (Over the years he has worked with Johnston & Murphy, Daniel Green, Golo and Sandler, to name a few.) I will take on accounts that are different than my own, and present a creative challenge. It gives me an opportunity to express myself in other areas. So far I haven't done anything in children's shoes, but I have some definite ideas and have talked about them, but so far I haven't done anything in the field. This area has great potential.

Where does a designer draw a line in accepting outside accounts?

"Really the only reward is doing a design that turns out to my satisfaction. I stop when the work is not carried out the way I want it. I've had dozens of offers from volume chain makers, but I don't understand the business, it isn't my cup of tea."

Should designers travel abroad for ideas?

"Such trips are important because they give you exposure. Dress designers go for the feeling and flair, not to copy. Creative people should go to Europe or to any place in the world to be inspired. Fashion is world wide and we should be aware of what's going on everywhere."

What is the difference between a designer and copyist?

"One has talent and the other has a good eye."

What do you do in your spare time?

"Nothing athletic. I love the theatre and arts and spend a lot of time in the Madison Avenue galleries. I collect paintings and sculpture, and I love to travel when I have time.

In a few words, why have you been successful?

"I don't punch a clock and I can't afford to be a prima donna. Most likely because I own my own business."

CHAPTER 23

Enthusiasm and Independence: Reasons for Success

Alan Goldstein

A~N~ exuberant individualist, who nevertheless delegates authority and delights in organizing (his own business, and Little League baseball, for two examples).

A confirmed independent—who serves in local trade associations and chairs footwear industry committees at the national level.

A man of physical energy finding release in hobbies of squash, hockey and golf. A thinker who likes to play bridge.

These are some aspects of the complex personality of Alan H. Goldstein, third-generation shoe man and 40-year-old president of Plymouth Shoe Co.

He is solidly-built, an Ivy League dresser, at the moment wearing long-wing brogues. His thoughts come out with a rush, punctuated by an occasional dead pause while he quickly gathers the precise words in which he wants to sum up an important idea. Suddenly the words dart off to capture some passing thought—then return unerringly to the point of departure.

"I'm a guy with ants in his pants," says Al Goldstein. "I can't sit still. I'm fundamentally impatient." But he sits quiet and relaxed in his chair as he says it. Only his face is continually moving from one expression to another, supplying emphasis to the steady flow of words.

Mentally, he has done little sitting still since he graduated from Dartmouth (Phi Beta Kappa) in 1947 to join his father's well-established men's shoe business. (The company's annual volume has risen from some $5.5 million at that time to about $10 million in 1966.) He credits Robert, his father, with excellence in selling and in fashion—two of his own outstanding interests.

"I love to sell," says Al Goldstein simply. "I could become glued to this chair and never get out of it. I believe this would be a mistake. I have never given up taking a serious share of selling in this company. We are sales-oriented. We believe strongly in an efficient productive setup, but unless cost dictates it we don't let factory control sales.

"We have a peculiar in-stock situation, a little different philosophy right or wrong. Having, say 12 sales representatives, we feel they should be the finest individuals possible;

they should be selling in their territories quite independently without controls.

"We require a minimum of control, for we feel we have intelligent young salesmen who can tell the customer where to place his money. If they're wrong, they can change. We don't want order-takers.

"We don't use a sales manager as such. Ray Draghetti, as vice-president for sales and styling, is an outstanding person. He's responsible for makeup salesmen and customer relations. I do the actual merchandising of the stock."

The giving of responsibility to qualified individuals carries throughout the company's operation. For example:

"After a nine-months' search we recently went outside the shoe industry to get a man with a professional engineering background in the electronics field. Our purpose was to go ahead within a framework of making quality shoes efficiently, using a fresh approach from outside."

But the control lines also converge in the hands of one individual:

"I'm not a great detail guy. I want the facts prepared. I want them put in front of me, and I have no qualms about making the decision. I like to look at the facts and make the answer.

"I'm not a professional manager. The value of the head of a small company is to project his personality on the company. We aim to be strong and flexible, and to run our business on a pro basis."

The flair for reorganization led to one major change in the Plymouth setup after the death of Robert Goldstein in 1962. And for a reason:

"We were at a sort of crossroads: In an industry where the big companies have an increasingly controlled distribution you're in a bad position without it. Also, from about

1955 to 1957, we'd been feeling the impact of imports. It was obvious that those who imported had benefits.

"We neither imported, nor had controlled distribution. How could an independent compete with people who had these two things?

"I felt we had to develop, so to speak, our own form of controlled distribution. One of our most serious problems was production peaks and valleys. The larger manufacturer could balance these better than we could.

"We brought both our manufacturing operations in Middleboro under the same roof at the main building here, and all the warehousing, supplies, and everything else into the other factory, and reorganized those quarters completely. Then, we said, we will put increasing emphasis on in-stock branded operations but also on the makeup—we would increase warehousing facility for those who were already warehousing under their own name, and we would encourage others to do so.

"This gave us a means of leveling production. We analyze the future: If things get tight we can increase the levels of warehousing and give people a chance to buy ahead.

"In 1964 we picked up an option to buy A. Freedman in New Bedford—a very successful makeup house that lent itself well to the type of operation and format we had developed. It fiitted into this warehousing servicing idea. So, we are looking both to build stock and increase makeup—but the branded operation is what we think important."

The only other plant acquisition has been the leasing, last fall, of a Harmony, Me., factory for additional output of handsewns, which Al Goldstein sees as staying in the picture for a long time. He displays no enthusiasm for mergers, no dreams of phenomenal growth:

"I'm realistic about this. I don't think I'm going to become an International, Genesco, or Brown, but I think this industry will still have need of the aggressive independent.

"I'd like to become a Hush Puppies—anybody would— but I'm not going to sit around waiting for it to happen. Maybe some day a group of us in New England will combine to form a single large company. But that's something for the future."

On the matter of imports, Mr. Goldstein is disposed to fight, rather than join.

Prominent on his office wall are group photos of the National Affairs Committee for the shoe manufacturing industry, headed by Mr. Goldstein, meeting with President Kennedy in October, 1963, and again with President Johnson the following April.

(The first picture bears an autograph of John Kennedy written, on request of his brother Ted from Massachusetts, the evening he was preparing to go to Dallas. It was received in the mail the day after the President's death. Nearby, by coincidence or otherwise, stands a sturdy antique rocking chair.)

"I think the work of this committee has resulted in this industry becoming one of the 10 most influential in Washington. We were able to sit down with 100 Congressmen and 35 Senators.

"One thing ought to be clear: This is not a drive solely directed toward orderly marketing and against imports. The primary purpose is to cover any situation and work with any situation, labeling or whatever, inviting action in Washington. Many areas need to be unified, and acted on.

"But—unless we get some form of orderly marketing act, imports will continue to increase. Today they're some 17 per cent. If we secure the Act in its present form (we're getting growing support from Missouri and Pennsylvania) I

think it will enable us to live with imports on an orderly
basis. It's the only way you can compete.

"One thing GALLS me"—for the first and only time during the interview one word is heavily stressed—"in conversations with Congressmen, importers, and retailers. It's the
imputation that style is the factor in the success of imports.
There is no monopoly in Europe, Japan, or Spain on creative imagination. The only monopoly they have is on low
price labor. We've proved that true time in and time out."

"Exports are not the answer. If you produce with labor
at over $2 an hour, and that's going into your product, how
will you sell to an individual who's earning 75 cents an
hour?

"The only answer to the import problem will be when we
can convince the retailer that he can sell more at higher
prices. That would be the greatest single factor that will give
us a greater margin to operate in."

"The Roper report pointed out that the consumer is too
satisfied with his shoes. You have to wonder if we may be
giving them too much, or if the prices are too low."

Al Goldstein launches into the subject of fashion by commenting on the work of the new men's fashion steering
committee set up at the last National Shoe Fair. (He is
chairman of this group, also of the Associated Fashion Service Men's shoe style committee—as well as a member of the
NSRA men's shoe style committee.)

"The idea is to sell more men's shoes by unifying the
entire industry—manufacturing, retailing, tanners, and most
important, clothing. So the ultimate consumer will suddenly
see in the form of advertising, window presentation and editorial comment, the concept of a shoe wardrobe coordinating
shoes with major areas of clothing.

"We feel the average American male has never been informed, stimulated and embarrassed into moving ahead. If antique brass is selected for brogues, everyone will have to get it.

"We must sell as independent companies but must sell the same thing. There will always be independent opportunities for competition between companies. But the first thing to worry about is to sell more shoes in total—then compete within that structure."

(Mr. Goldstein is asked to elaborate on an earlier statement that after the American male reaches age 21, the number of shoes he buys drops off dramatically.)

"Obviously there's no question that the average youngster, even though he might not have any financial resources up to age 21 or so, spends more for his clothing and is more conscious of what is taking place in the world of fashion than he will be at age 25.

"They're gregarious and want to dress like everyone else. If I walk through a clothing or shoe department with my teenage son, or daughter, they will recognize every item, name every color; they'll know which ones the other kids are getting and which shoe they wear with which garment.

"Of course teenagers wear out clothing quicker, but also they want cranberry or whatever is new, regardless of what else they already have. The retailers develop this attitude and continuously change their merchandise because the tastes are so volatile. And the kids keep buying, and their dads keep paying.

"Now when this kid gets married, or gets a grown-up job, his shoe buys drop off by three pairs, and the basic reason for that is not financial.

"He realizes now he's in a different category—say business. We have not made this category into a place where it's impossible to get away with not wearing the right shoes.

"This guy is still gregarious and wants to dress right—which he does from the ankles up. We want to create an atmosphere where if he doesn't buy the right shoe he will feel out of place. If he attempts to go to a formal party without formal shoes he should be made to feel like a fool. Not that brogues are okay just because they're black.

"We've got to give this man a wardrobe sense—formal shoes with formal wear, casuals with casual wear, slippers with pajamas, dress shoes with a business suit, and so on.

"If we can get him to buy just one more pair for one more outfit, we'll have a 33⅓ per cent increase for the industry."

Mr. Goldstein stresses one essential point about fashion: it is evolutionary, not revolutionary:

"The biggest mistake we could make would be to create a radical new type before people are ready for it. Fashion is not 'way out'—it is a total package. When they get up to four or five pairs, then we can get more radical.

"Here's an example of evolution: In brogues and hand-sewn mocs generally, this season and the one before, there has been a growing interest and demand for colors as against black—olives, antique brasses, natural tones that we call bonanza or palomino.

"This to me would indicate a growing trend toward colors with lighter tones. Therefore we won't put out a group of colors reverting to dark tones. We'll have a group even lighter, which we will call surf sands.

"Also, we don't just repeat what has been successful. If you find long-wing brogues are so damn good, it's not a matter of just making more of them. You have to come up with an idea of what makes them attractive, find out what's the appeal of them. Then take it from there. Determine the direction things are going in, then develop items to take you in that direction.

"Styling also calls for balance, in two ways: First, the shoe must have balance within itself—a feeling for over-all appearance, outline, relation of one part to another. It's ridiculous to have a light, trim top, then put a heavy, thick bottom on it.

"The other point is balance of the shoe with the wardrobe. Why are brogues and wing tips wrong with formal wear? The whole appearance of formal apparel today is neat and trim. We should design sleek and neat looking shoes to go with it.

"Suppose you want to tie in with corduroy jackets. You don't just make a corduroy shoe to wear with it. You think what is the character of that jacket? Perhaps you decide, 'it's rough.' Then you get a feeling for roughness into the shoe, with appropriate leathers and patterns.

"How do you get good styling? You can't teach it, it has to be born in you. Then, a lot of discussion and analysis— getting rapport with apparel people, tanners, customers. Then we sit down and translate these ideas into designs, then tell our resources what we want in patterns, last, leathers, et cetera.

"Another example of evolution is the history of our 'Stowaway.' We had been seeing each year a demand for glovier types—we felt this was a must for getting the casual look. But the trouble was: We had been trying to give existing styles a soft feeling through those types of leather.

"Then a resource came to us with a shoe designed for hot rodders, with a rubber sole wrapped up the back. The style was an espadrille, which we adapted into a handsewn.

"This shoe bombed. The retailers liked it but it just didn't sell. We asked what was wrong.

"We decided it was not the outline, not the leathers—the soling was too extreme. What to do?"

"We kept the outline, changed to crepe, cushion crepe and chrome leather soles; took the extreme design off the back, came out with new glove leathers and new colors. Now the shoe has sold many thousand pairs and we know this is going to be a big shoe. This came about in an evolutionary way."

What does Al Goldstein see as the current direction in styling?

"The biggest: Toward more casual footwear, softer types of leathers. One reason for handsewns being so big is because they are casual.

"In all categories: More color acceptance.

"Toward heavier shoes, moving along with the bolder, heavier look in the clothing industry.

"Lasts: More square and modified square toes, also flatter."

How long will these trends continue?

"These things usually go in a 3-to-5-year cycle, like clothing."

Has he any forecast beyond that point?

"If I can be right about what will be good next year, I'll be happy. If I can see for the next 2 years, I'll be delighted. If I can see beyond that, I'd be a genius.

"But in that case I wouldn't be in the shoe business any more. I'd be in the stock market."